D1113198

"In her charming debut . . . [Hanlon] turns the quotidian details of marriage and family life into a lyrical investigation of 'something bigger and more complex than oneself.' . . . Merging leisurely seaside adventure with ecological sensibilities, Hanlon delivers a lyrical ode to a changing environment."
—*Publishers Weekly*

"[Hanlon] is as skilled at demystifying complex scientific concepts as she is in portraying gold-spangled waterline sunsets and muted winter compositions of marsh grasses. The whole is enriched with personal reflections on raising a family, aging, and the changing nature of marriage."
—*Foreword Reviews*

SWIMMING
TO THE TOP
OF THE TIDE

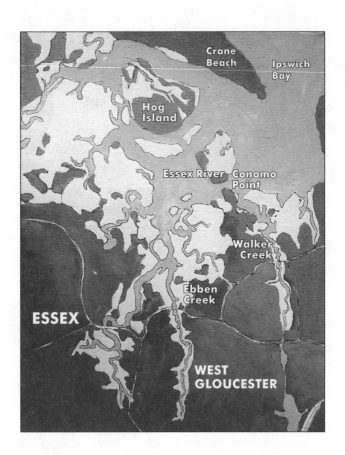

SWIMMING TO THE TOP OF THE TIDE

Finding Life Where Land and Water Meet

Patricia Hanlon

Bellevue Literary Press
NEW YORK

First published in the United States in 2021
by Bellevue Literary Press, New York

For information, contact:
Bellevue Literary Press
90 Broad Street
Suite 2100
New York, NY 10004
www.blpress.org

Library of Congress Cataloging-in-Publication Data
Names: Hanlon, Patricia, author.
Title: Swimming to the top of the tide : finding life where land and water meet /
    Patricia Hanlon.
Description: First edition. | New York : Bellevue Literary Press, 2021. |
    Includes bibliographical references.
Identifiers: LCCN 2020035027 (print) | LCCN 2020035028 (ebook) |
    ISBN 9781942658870 (paperback) | ISBN 9781942658887 (epub)
Subjects: LCSH: Salt marsh ecology—New England. | Marsh ecology—
    Conservation—New England.
Classification: LCC QH104.5.N4 H36 2021 (print) | LCC QH104.5.N4 (ebook) |
    DDC 577.690974—dc23
LC record available at https://lccn.loc.gov/2020035027
LC ebook record available at https://lccn.loc.gov/2020035028

Bellevue Literary Press would like to thank all its generous donors—individuals and
foundations—for their support.

 This publication is made possible by the New York State
Council on the Arts with the support of Governor Andrew
M. Cuomo and the New York State Legislature.

Book design and composition by Mulberry Tree Press, Inc.

Bellevue Literary Press is committed to ecological stewardship in our book
production practices, working to reduce our impact on the natural environment.

♾ This book is printed on acid-free paper.

Manufactured in the United States of America.

First Edition

9 8 7 6 5 4 3 2 1

paperback ISBN: 978-1-942658-87-0
ebook ISBN: 978-1-942658-88-7

For our children and grandchildren

We shape the world by living.

—Jedediah Purdy, *After Nature: A Politics for the Anthropocene*

CONTENTS

12   *Contents*

SWIMMING
TO THE TOP
OF THE TIDE

LAND AND SEA:
AN OVERTURE

With our extended family now scattered across five states, my husband, Robert, and I fly more often than we used to. If it's a daytime flight, we book seats in consecutive rows, so we're near each other but have our own window seats. If he's in the seat ahead, I talk to the edge of his face: the back of his ear, a bit of graying hair, the slight curve of an eyelash. If he's behind me and I've gotten absorbed in some reading, I might feel a nudge (or vice versa).

Look, that nudge says. *Something interesting down below.*

Not so long ago, on a cloudless spring day, we flew back to Boston from Tampa. After crossing upper Florida, the plane followed the coast and we had the rare treat of watching a thousand-some miles of continental edge—all the way from Georgia to Massachusetts—scroll by down below like a story.

Along the coast of Georgia and the Carolinas, that story unfolds at a leisurely pace. Rivers flow seaward. The sea, with its twice-daily tides, pushes back. Matter is shaken up and rearranged, but the whole thing stays more or less in balance, sustaining a permanently impermanent coastal band of thresholds facing both ways: watery land and "landy" water.

North of Charleston, South Carolina, there is a subtle change in the shape of the coastline. It begins to "scallop," with the pointy parts, the spits and shoals, facing more dramatically seaward. There's a pronounced swoop from Myrtle Beach to Frying Pan Shoals, in North Carolina, then another one beginning at the sand spit near Harkers Island, where the intertidal zone swells out into the Atlantic like a pregnant belly, forming the combined Pamlico and Albemarle Sounds.

Another shift occurs near Virginia Beach, where the continental-edge story begins happening on a more epic scale. The interfingerings of land and sea coalesce into much larger "innies" and "outies," like the Chesapeake and Delaware Bays, separated by the Delmarva Peninsula.

The East Coast turns a corner at the slender barrier spit of Sandy Hook, near the New Jersey–New York state line. This is also where the Laurentide Ice Sheet halted twenty thousand years ago, before beginning its long retreat. From here on up, the coast shows the influence of glacial flow and ebb. The shoreline includes exposed bedrock, deep natural harbors, and large rivers reaching deeper inland. Just past Sandy Hook is the New Jersey–New York Harbor. Unlike the vast salt marshes of the

South, the ones here are fewer and farther apart, tucked between rocky coasts and urban hardscape.

Toward the end of that flight, I must have nodded off, because when Robert nudged me, we'd flown past Boston and were forty miles north of the city, in a holding pattern. At one mile above sea level instead of five, waves now unfurled, boats cut through the water, and cars slid like beads on the highways. While I hadn't been watching, the view out the window had become much more local—our local, in fact. The plane banked, the porthole briefly framing a thousand-some acres of tidal estuary sheltered by the two barrier beaches we know well, Wingaersheek and Crane.

For just that instant, it appeared to be its own little planet, perfect, whole, self-evident.

In the forty-plus years we have lived here and raised a family, we've explored these waterways, first in an eighteen-foot sailboat, then a fourteen-foot motorboat, and, later, slender ocean kayaks. But it wasn't until our three children were grown and had become visitors in our lives that we started regularly swimming the estuary's creeks and channels. Over the years, our boats had become smaller and smaller, until finally our own bodies—altered slightly with gear—became our main watercraft.

We made a pact with each other to swim every time we possibly could. After a summer idyll of blue skies and marshes as lush as Kansas cornfields, we swam later and later into the fall, matching the dropped temperatures with heavier wetsuits, boots, and gloves. We took for granted that we'd eventually hit a wall that would stop the swimming until the ocean warmed up again the following year. But as we swam in rain, darkness, and, a few times, slushy water just above freezing, we discovered that walls are relative. Or, as Robert declared one night, stoking the fire, "Walls have doors. Or if you can't find the door, you can go around it." Even the coldest and stormiest conditions were navigable with the right gear and the mutual desire to be there. As we swam into the winter and then into a spring that was agonizingly long in coming, the practice became what Wendell Berry has called a "journey of one inch, very arduous and humbling and joyful, by which we arrive at the ground at our own feet, and learn to be at home."

Part 1 of this book is the chronology of a particular year, from July 2008 to the following summer. It's about exploring the same landscape over and over, noticing more and more about its materials and its creatures, its cycles and patterns and processes. It's about the vibrant energy of a place where two ecologies blend, jostle, and bring forth new life.

But prolonged exposure to an estuary also reveals the human interventions that have affected this critically important ecosystem, the disconnects and disruptions. Part 2 is necessarily less linear; it is a citizen-scientist's attempt to understand—through the lens of my own local environment—something of our current cultural and evolutionary moment, with both its tragedies and its possibilities. It is about how the habit became, as the philosopher David Abram has put it, "a dialogue where the environment puts questions to the organism and the organism, in answering those questions, puts new questions to the environment. The environment, in turn, answers with further questions."

A final note: I say "we" a lot here. In part that's because outdoor swimming is generally a buddy-system sport, especially during New England's cold months. And fellow travelers can, at times, function as a kind of two-brained, four-eyed observing organism. Much of what I have recorded here exists in a matrix of shared experience, and retains that texture.

PART 1

For unless one is "placed"
one merely collects sensations
as a sightseer, lacking the local knowledge
that grounds and measures global knowledge.

—Gerald W. Schlabach, "The Vow of Stability:
A Premodern Way through a Hypermodern World"

BEDROCK

You don't have to look far anywhere on Cape Ann to see granite. You find it in the craggy upthrusts that form the Cape's high places: Poles Hill, Mount Ann, Red Rock, Thompson Mountain. Along the northeast-facing coast, constant wave action has exposed it and polished it to a lapidary beauty. But in the sparsely populated interior of the Cape, you can actually climb down *into* granite bedrock by visiting the pits—now beautiful pools—left behind by the quarrying industry.

Our swimming practice began here, in the Cape's rocky interior. We were taking a week-long vacation at home, hoping to revisit local places we'd known over the years but mostly, these days, just passed on our way to somewhere else. We were squarely in midlife, with demanding fulltime jobs and children in college.

Day three was especially hot and humid, and we were on our way to the property of friends of ours, where we have a standing invitation to swim anytime. Harry and Judith live about half a mile inland from the seaside town of Lanesville, up a winding gravel road, and have two small pits on their property.

We pulled into their driveway and got out, towels slung over our shoulders, both of us in old, infrequently used bathing suits: faded plaid trunks for Robert, a nondescript black tank suit for me. All quiet except for the whistling of the breeze through the scrubby pines, the slap of our sandals on powdery dirt.

Picture a hundred-foot-long lap pool, but with mineral green water reminiscent of mountain cirque lakes. One side of the pit is formed by a vertical purplish gray granite wall; the other, by a long, very regularly shaped rock pile, which intersects the water at about a forty-five-degree angle. This pit is spring-fed and stays mostly in shadow, so even on a hot summer day, it's quite cold. There's no good reason to enter it gradually. Robert had already leaped ahead, and I was close behind, letting out an involuntary shriek as the chill hit my skin.

I stayed on the sunny strip along the side of the grout pile, the gray-and-white-speckled stones magnified underwater. I reached the end of the quarry and reversed direction. It was colder coming back because we'd stirred up the thin top layer of slightly warmer water. Robert was ahead, floating on his back.

A few laps later, we got out, shivering even in the ninety-degree heat. We climbed back up the chute to the grassy path that led to the second quarry, a larger one fully exposed to sunlight. It felt like a bathtub, relatively speaking. I swam languid circles, surrounded by the rose- and caramel-colored granite walls. Tiny fish darted in and out of sunny spots in the water. I was in no hurry to get out, but Robert swam a few laps and headed for the shore and the sloping lawn of our friends' yard.

"I'll be back," he said, drying off, draping his towel over a lawn chair uphill from the pit. He pulled on his shorts, stepped into his shoes, and disappeared onto one of the paths branching out from the quarry into the woods. I knew he'd be flicking stones and snapping overhanging branches from the trail as he went, in order to make an easier way for the next person. This autopilot trail maintenance is as much a part of his gait as the specific swing of his arms.

Just as I was beginning to think about getting out, I spotted a pair of swim fins that had been tucked into a cleft in the rock. They were torn in a few places and had been patched together with duct tape, but they fit okay. I slipped back into the water and swam to the far end of the quarry, then back again in what seemed like seconds. The fins gave each kick extra length and leverage, like a powerful new body part.

It had taken me all of a minute to spot the fins, swim to them, slip them on, and experience the results. But hundreds more swims were contained in that intersection of chance and human choice.

On the way home, we stopped at a dive shop in downtown Gloucester and bought three pairs of fins—two for us and one for Judith, a thank-you gift.

RIVER BASIN

A mile north of our friends' quarries is a rocky jut called Halibut Point, one of many capes within the Cape. Here the intertidal band is narrow, and water meets land confrontationally. Inky waves split against orange granite; whitewater surges in and out of crevasses in the rocks like a washing machine on heavy-duty cycle. The only species that can survive the constant pounding and scouring are the barnacles and snails and starfish, the chitons and anemones and sea urchins. The enormous energy of the waves, powered by the gravitational tug of the Moon and the Earth, never lets up. It's a dangerous place to swim, a violent place for creatures without shells or suction cups.

Just a few miles away, though, at Wingaersheek Beach, the intertidal region is gently elongated. It involves the same overall wave force that pushes the breakers at Halibut Point, but here it's attenuated, softened. That fizzing sound you hear when you are knee-deep in gentle surf, your lungs full of salt air, is millions of small collisions of water against tiny grains of silica, millions of air bubbles bursting in rapid succession. Creatures living in

these shallow, sandy waters must be able to swim or burrow, since not a single sand grain stays in one place for
very long. The burrowers—the clams and crabs—must
also be able to filter-feed, straining the ocean water for
plankton and detritus.

If you walk to the northern tip of Wingaersheek—
several miles from the public entrance to the private
end of the beach—you will see the tip of Crane Beach
up ahead. These two barrier beaches come within a few
hundred feet of each other, creating a deep channel, or
"hole," where an enormous volume of seawater flows in
and out of the Essex River Basin twice each day. The
watery boundaries of three towns—Gloucester, Essex,
and Ipswich—converge here in what is often called
the Essex Bay, but the more geographically accurate
name is the Essex River Basin. At high tide it does
look like a bay, but at low tide the sandbars and sand
flats turn into islands, and the river's path through the
basin is clear.

The day after the quarry swim, we headed down a
private drive off Concord Street in West Gloucester. It
was a bumpy ride on a single-lane gravel road edged by
cedar, scrubby red pine, and dramatic outcroppings of
granite. The road forked like a bird's foot, each toe leading to a different promontory of land. We followed the
middle fork, which led to a parking area in a shadowy
glade of cedar trees. One of the perks of living in the

same place for decades is that you gain an encyclopedic knowledge of where you can trespass and where you can't.

We emerged from semidarkness into humid brightness and a sweeping view of the Essex River Basin. It was an hour or two away from low tide, and the water had distilled to a few looping channels. Docks stood at steep angles. We made our way down boulders covered with slippery ocher seaweed, pausing at the water's edge. When the channel was clear of boat traffic as far as we could see or hear in either direction, we pulled on our fins and slid into the briskly flowing current, entering in real life one of those word problems that were the bane of my adolescence: If a current is moving eastward at a certain rate, and you wish to travel across to the sand flats on the other side, at what angle and velocity must you swim?

I was stroking hard, aiming west even as I was pulled due east—it felt like a combination of swimming and skidding on ice. Robert's head appeared, disappeared, and then reappeared in the chop. "Don't get pulled into the chute," he yelled, meaning the fifty-foot-deep strait between the tips of Crane and Wingaersheek beaches, where swells were breaking over an offshore sandbar and roiling the channel.

The fins were a necessity now. Like any lever, they multiplied the unaided force of the human body, allowing me to push against a strong, buckling current that otherwise would have overwhelmed my foot and thigh muscles.

We just made it into the shallower, gentler current that ran between the back side of Crane—all chalk white sand and heathery swaths of dune grass—and the high-walled east coast of this vast sand flat. We found an inlet and scrambled up, pulling off our fins and tossing them up onto land. As I straightened and stood, my heart was still racing, spots pulsing in my field of vision. To the northeast of Crane Beach lay the distinctively drumlin-shaped Hog Island (also known as Choate Island), blue-green with densely planted Norway spruce. To the west and south, the low, wooded hills of Essex and West Gloucester. The tapered end of Wingaersheek completed the circle.

We set out, our bare feet meeting hard ribs of sand in places where the tide had receded rapidly, and sinking into soft places where the water had moved more slowly. We loomed over rivulets moving chaotically in different directions. We forded a channel that bisected the bar like a waist-deep Mississippi River.

We reached the western side of the flats, its California. Conomo Point, a summer colony five miles by road from where we'd parked our car, seemed close enough to swim to. Farther away, between Conomo Point and Hog Island, we could make out a string of small motorboats hauled up on a long, sandy, muddy spit, and men bent over, wielding their clam forks in search of the soft-shell clams (*Mya arenaria*) that are the signature species of our area. We'd dug them ourselves a few times. Holes and squirting water mean "clams at home," so that's where you'd wield your clam fork. Fork still inserted, you'd pull back a slab of mud and remove any embedded clams. But professional clammers break far fewer shells than we do.

On the rising side of the tide's bell curve, the boats would be in navigable water again and the clammers would head into town, where they have arrangements with local restaurants and shellfish companies. Unlike the summer people at the Point, when they're zipping around in their boats, they're commuting, not pleasure-boating.

Across the channel, near where we'd started out, something shimmered intermittently—one of Bill Wainwright's outdoor kinetic sculptures, made of steel, aluminum, and reflective surface coverings. Even far out in the Ipswich Bay you can often make out "Essex Light," a daytime star uncommonly close to Earth.

We drove home by way of Concord Street, which threads together the juts and inlets of the coast. On our landward side were West Gloucester's rugged uplands, once divided into large tracts for seventeenth- and eighteenth-century homesteads and farms.

But humans had been living in these parts long before the newly incorporated town of Gloucester handed out land grants to the Coffins and Coles and Herricks and Haskells. Genetically modern humans had, in fact, arrived in New England some twelve thousand years ago. It was a pivotal time: The Laurentide glacier was retreating north into Canada, and small groups of spear-hunting nomads roamed what was then still semiarctic tundra, chasing caribou and woolly mammoths. It was the dawn of what we now call the Holocene epoch, that arc of time, continuing into the present, when *Homo sapiens* began colonizing the planet both by its cultural and technological innovations and by its sheer numbers.

During the Late Woodland period (between three thousand and five hundred years ago), Cape Ann rejoined the Temperate Zone, and was inhabited by the Algonquin. With Arctic big game long gone, they had become farmers of corn, pumpkins, rye, beans, and squash. They hunted deer and other woodland game; they fished for cod, mackerel, herring, and bass. They dug clams for the meat and used the shells as tools. Salt-marsh hay insulated their houses and fed their livestock. They made arrow shafts, baskets, and other household items from the reeds that grew in brackish zones. In short, they adapted to the contours and materials of a particular bit of coastland at a particular evolutionary moment. Their impact on the land was minimal.

The first colonists continued the Indians' subsistence farming, hunting, and fishing out of necessity. Yet they'd brought with them some of the tools and, even more important, the mindset of late-Renaissance England, where agriculture had been boosted by waterpower for centuries. It was not long after the initial settlement of Cape Ann that the colonists began constructing their own water-powered mills. When William Haskell surveyed Walker Creek in the late 1600s, he may have paused to take in its beauty, but it's fair to assume he mostly saw the creek as a source of food, a means of travel, and a way to harness the energy needed to turn a mill wheel—greatly reducing the effort and multiplying the yield of what one person could do with a mortar and pestle. Upriver, where water flowed down from the West Gloucester hills into the creek, Haskell's neighbor Henry Walker was running a sawmill, processing the area's pine and white oak into clapboards, hoops, and staves, as well as the ribs and planking for boats.

We'd paused on the bridge, engine idling. I caught a whiff of dank marsh mud, a hint of sulphur. Now at dead low tide, Walker Creek was little more than a tea-colored ribbon winding through mud.

At high tide the neighborhood kids have always cooled off here, leaping off the stub of plank wedged under the bridge railing, getting swept by the current under the bridge to the other side, and then scrambling up the stone embankments to do it all over again.

To our left was the dock that had belonged to the poet Peter Davison, the gable end of his yellow Georgian Colonial just visible behind a stand of cedar trees. Another car approached up ahead, and we pulled over the bridge to let them by.

This area has stayed quiet. Small farms here never scaled up much beyond providing for a single household. There was nowhere, really, to expand operations: All the tillable land is squeezed between puzzle pieces of marsh and swamp and ledge. The area was too far from open water to compete with Gloucester proper as a fishing port, or with Essex as a shipbuilding empire. Haskell's gristmill ground its last corn somewhere around 1860, and Walker's sawmill ceased operations not long after.

The railroad from Boston to Gloucester, completed in 1846, brought not only cheaper goods from far away but also tourists to the Cape. In 1852, the first summerhouses appeared at Coffin's Beach. During the twentieth century, Bostonians built second homes on the water side of Concord Street; tradespeople built year-round houses on the landward side.

Over the course of the twentieth century, more and more former farmland was subdivided, including some acreage west of Sumner Street, bought in 1940 by one Charles Newman. His son Merrill, known as "Tink," sold us five acres of that land in 1979. We met and became friends with other couples, all of us baby boomers or a little older. Though we sometimes fished for stripers, dug for clams, and gathered up marsh hay for mulching our gardens, we did not actually need these riches of the marshland ecosystem to survive.

TIDAL STRAIT

The next day we were back in the water, possible museum visits and other vacation plans set aside. This time, we stood on the sun-warmed planks of the public dock at Conomo Point, watching pleasure boats putt through the "No Wake" zone. A cabin cruiser pulled up alongside the dock to let out sunburned, sandy passengers. When the lull in boat traffic came, we slid into the turbulent passage between the Point and Cross Island. In the middle of the channel, we were swept into a small whirlpool, a churning ring of current surrounding a flat, smooth oval, the water equivalent of the eye of a hurricane. I yelped, backpedaling, but was swung around like in a game of crack the whip, then shot out on the other side.

Reaching the shoreline of Cross Island, we made our way against the current by clutching seaweed and barnacle-encrusted rocks. The face of the island was sheer granite, sea-foam green lichen at the top edging into a peachy orange, a horizontal zone above the water most of the time. Then a sooty orange at the mean tide line. At the low-tide line, the rocks were a glistening black, skirted with kelp.

Half swimming, half crawling, we spotted a great blue heron up ahead on the rocks at the waterline, watching for fish in the current flowing from around the bend in the island. Gunmetal blue with a white head, it stood about three and a half feet tall, its spearlike yellow bill poised downward. We approached slowly, not kicking now, just pulling forward on our elbows, barnacles scraping our palms and forearms. The current combed over the rocks and parted around our bodies.

Far above the waterline, a banded kingfisher perched on the branch of a dead tree, peering down, waiting for dinner to appear in its crosshairs. It shot up into the air and hurled itself down into the water like a spear, emerging a few seconds later with a small, flapping fish.

Meanwhile, the heron had not budged. But it had finally noticed us. You can hold a gaze for a long time with a cat or dog, but a wild animal is another story: The animal is always the first to break away. We crawled closer, till we were just a few feet away and could practically count the feathers in the black plumes running from just above its eye to the back of its head. Finally, the heron lifted off and flew away across the channel, a lumbering flight, landing on a pile of rocks on the opposite shore.

We headed back, borne along with the current. The

receding tide had exposed a mussel bed near the dock—dark, dense clusters of them covering the rocks.

Unlike clams, mussels don't hide from you. We quickly filled the mesh bag Robert had brought along. Wet mussels are a glistening blue-black, their smooth, slightly pear-shaped shells scored with fine concentric growth lines—like tree rings. They are lovely to hold, a satisfying heft in your palm. Before slipping them in the bag, we tested each one, pressing the shells together; the dead ones full of mud easily slide apart. The largest were about three inches long.

We were feeling the cold. After nearly an hour, it was time to get out. Even in July, you don't warm up swimming the way you would if you were running. We reached the dock and heaved ourselves up. Water streaming down his body, Robert plucked up the towels we'd left near our shoes, and tossed me one.

"I've heard you can swim even into the first part of October around here," he said, drying off his head and putting his glasses back on.

"We could," I said, wrapping my towel around my torso, slipping into my flip-flops.

"Well, I'm not going to be the one to quit."

Back home, Robert rinsed the bagful of mussels with the garden hose, then shook them from the bag into our kitchen sink, which I'd filled with water—to give the mussels a chance to filter out sand inside their shells. Rechecking each mussel to make sure it was tightly shut,

I tugged off the "beard," the cluster of threads protruding from the hinge of the shell. The sink water swirled with bits of seaweed and stray barnacles. A fine layer of sand covered the bottom of the sink.

After pouring an inch of white wine into a heavy pot, Robert transferred the mussels from the sink to the pot and shut the lid. The smell of wine and garlic filled the kitchen.

I sliced a single large tomato into translucent red wedges, then set the table. Because there are just two of us most of the time, our dinner table is our kitchen island, where we sit on tall stools facing each other. The island's top is a piece of gray-and-white marble. It makes an attractive matrix for plates, glasses, and candles. Against the backdrop of the marble, with its clouds and swirls and faint lightning bolts, these objects form the stage set on which our dinners are enacted each night. And Robert and I are the human subjects among the ritual objects.

We feasted on meat that ranged in size from a quarter to a silver dollar; in color, from white to tan to russet. The meat was mild and sweet like scallops, piquant with bits of garlic.

As we ate and talked, the world outside the kitchen window darkened; candle wax pooled and spilled. The pile of empty shells grew, iridescent with the same substance, nacre, that also coats the outsides of pearls.

"We could live on these," Robert said.

After dinner, I gathered up the shells and dumped them outside in an inconspicuous spot where they would shed their last bits of flesh and, over time, become pure calcium. We would add them to our driveway of crushed shells.

I had set several mussels aside that were opened up a little too far to be safe to eat. They had a faint pungence that may or may not have signaled decomposition. I have a visceral horror of seeing any creature in the throes of dying, but something made me pry one open. Splayed like a pinned butterfly, it was all glistening sushi colors, the flesh completely filling the shell. The pale orange mantle attached to the edges of each valve cradled the visceral mass, the animal's soft metabolic region: stomach, lungs, intestine, heart, kidney. The magenta foot lay limp. I felt I wasn't done looking, so I put it in a small bowl, covered it with water, and left it in an inconspicuous place in the kitchen.

The next evening we went back to the dive shop and bought gloves. Our hands were scraped from gripping barnacle-covered rocks, and Robert had the additional challenge of arthritis in his hands—it was important that they stay warm. While we were there, we also tried on—and ended up buying—ankle-length, sleeveless "Farmer John" wetsuits, long-sleeve pullover wetsuit tops, and water socks thin enough to easily fit inside our fins.

My nose remembered the bowl several days later. Grimacing, I poured off the cloudy water, flushed the softly decomposing meat down the toilet, and rinsed the shell. All that was left of the creature was its scaffolding: The sinewy adductor muscles, which had been the shell's gatekeepers, relaxing to open it and contracting to close it back up. The gasket-like strip lining the outer edge of the shell. A few "beard" threads remained, too. These were the belaying line that the mussel had produced from its byssal gland, and used to lasso itself to rocks, pier pilings, and—because these are (in some sense) relational creatures—a neighborhood of other mussels.

EBBEN CREEK

At each rising tide, the Essex River splits into tributaries that meander deep into the uplands of West Gloucester, Essex, and Ipswich. Some untold tonnage of seawater passes in and out of these tidal creeks twice a day, saturating the peaty marshlands, filling them like sponges, working an array of biogeochemical magic. It's a diffuse, squishy, soggy meeting between land and sea, a leisurely approach that nurtures life in innumerable soft, fecund places—the yin, perhaps, to Halibut Point's yang. Here the intertidal zone can stretch for miles.

As anyone who's ever bought a gym membership knows, it's one thing to start a practice. Keeping one going takes not just desire but also identifying and confronting the obstacles. I adjusted my work schedule to leave more time in the evenings to swim, and we also swam closer to home. If it was around low tide in the evening, we went to Conomo Point, just two miles away from our front door, where there was always water deep enough for swimming.

Evening high tides, though, opened up a wonderful opportunity to swim the tidal creeks. Closest to

home at the time was Ebben Creek, named for Ebenezer Burnham, a nineteenth-century boatbuilder. It
passes under Route 133, a well-traveled state highway. Just off the highway, tourists wait in long lines
for fried seafood at Farnham's ("Famous for Fried
Clams"). The view from the picnic tables is a wide
swath of the Essex River Basin, with upper Ebben
Creek zigzagging picturesquely northeast toward
Hog Island. This is the iconic view of the marsh, the
view that turns up in Google Earth snapshots and in
paintings by local landscape artists attracted by the
lush beauty and the strong diagonals.

The landward side of the creek, on the other
hand, doesn't attract much attention from either artists or the Farnham's crowd. A few turns and Ebben
appears to vanish into a soft, indefinite landscape of
marsh edged by woods.

One August evening, we ventured into the creek's
"B side," stepping over a steel guardrail onto a sparse
lawn. A passing semitrailer downshifted with a tuba-
sounding rumble; the smell of fried food mingled with
licorice whiffs of hot asphalt. Downhill a few feet more
and the land grass gave way to *Spartina patens,* commonly known as marsh hay. (*Spartina alterniflora*, marsh
cordgrass, is coarser and taller, and grows in the marsh's
lower elevations, often lining the channels.) The incoming current surged and buckled. We were swept out into
the choppy, sparkling middle of the channel. Our bodies

instinctively took on aspects of animals' navigation: the powerful back legs of a frog, the torso swivel of a dolphin, the flutter of a fish's tail.

The ocean-chilled current carried us a hundred feet or so before it fanned out and began to blend with water that had been heating up all day in the sun. Farnham's shrank, and the traffic sounds softened, absorbed into the great warm mass of mud, water, and vegetation. The creek herringboned around my outstretched arm, reflecting the saturated blue of the sky, the vertical slashes of grass lining the channel.

We floated past the backyard of a small raised ranch house, where a woman (too far up to see us) paused for a moment behind a push mower. After that, we passed a 1970s A-frame with a satellite dish. One more house, its backyard deck barely visible through cedar trees, and then it was just the creek snaking through fields.

Snaking is the operative word for how a tidal creek cuts through a flat land at sea level, veering around obstacles rather than over them. Swimming these meanderings, we retraced the geological history of sediment deposited and worn away with the twice-daily tides.

Another sharp turn brought us to a grassy promontory and a fifty-foot-tall oak tree.

"Red-tailed hawk," Robert said, pointing to a broad-winged bulk on a branch near the top. Not far from the hawk, a turkey vulture was circling.

"They're watching us," I said.

"We must be moving too slowly to look healthy."

We rounded increasingly circuitous bends. Turning a corner, we surprised a cormorant, which immediately dove beneath the water to avoid us. Two bends later, like bulls in this ecological china shop, we disturbed the peace of two white egrets.

We were floating barely forward, watching the flecks of marsh grass and air bubbles on the water's surface slow down and finally pause. All but the top foot or so of the marsh grass was flooded. The stillness pulsed with life sounds normally too faint to hear: the beating of birds' wings, the drowsy hum of a jet, the slight tinnitus that has been with me as long as I can remember, a mind event that skates the edge between real and unreal.

Some time later—three minutes? seven?—a single air bubble drifted past my nose, seaward. My suspended body began floating seaward, too. I flicked a fin, swiveled onto my front again. Robert, too. Our bodies grazed.

(A lot can be said about marriage, but fundamentally it has to do with two human bodies in close proximity over many years. From time to time as you're borne along, you catch and hold a gaze, regarding each other from a foot away, twenty feet, an inch or less. Years ago, when we were courting, testing out the edges between friendship and romance, I could not hold the gaze for long. It was too soon. There was not enough "there" yet between us.)

As we retraced the creek's hairpin turns and bow

bends, the water level dropped, the change barely perceptible at first, then revealing a bit of glistening waterline
on the cordgrass. More and more of the grass resurfaced,
along with the tops of the creek's mud walls, exposing
their erosion-formed juts and hollows.

Around another bend, the Farnham's sign reappeared.

Back at the bridge, we pulled off our fins in the
water, tossing them up on the shore. We hoisted ourselves up onto wet rocks, watching for slippery spots
as we clambered up out of meandering geological time
and back into cars streaking by and people crossing the
street and an amplified voice calling out an order ready
for pickup: "Sixty-two! Sixty-two!"

In the hour we'd been in the water, the tide had
dropped half a foot. The customers and cars that were
at Farnham's when we set out had been replaced with
new ones.

The power lines buzzed faintly, an electromagnetic
phenomenon called "corona discharge." My heartbeat
pinged in my ears. It is a fact that the human circula-
tory system looks strikingly like an aerial view of an
estuary's branching channels and countless tiny capil-
laries. We had, in fact, traveled down one such tiny
capillary, toward the farthest and subtlest instances of
land meeting sea.

TIDELOG

The arc of daylight shrinks by about one-third from the summer solstice to the fall equinox. On the first of September, sunset had been at 7:17, dark at 8:20. By the end of the month, the sun would set at 6:26, and darkness would fall at 7:27. Even in early September, we'd have only a small window of time after I arrived home from work—usually by 5:30—and before dark. But that window would shrink even further as the month progressed.

I knew all of this because of the Tidelog Robert uses as his date book. It shows not just high and low tides but also sunrise and sunset, moonrise and moonset. All of that information is available elsewhere, but the Tidelog provides it all in a snapshot: two bell curves for each day, representing the swell and fall of the tide, one slightly larger than the other, like two uneven breasts. Sometimes the tallest tide was the earlier one, sometimes the later.

I liked thumbing through it like a flip-book, watching the slow swell from neap to superhigh full-moon tides, which in our area can reach twelve and a half feet above the mean low tide level. I learned to read a steep curve as more water than usual moving in and out of the bay in the same amount of time. That meant a stronger than normal current, and barely a pause between incoming and outgoing tides. A less steep curve, on the other hand, represented a more leisurely pace, a longer pause at the top of the tide. These are all things you want to know in great detail if you are actually down *in* the tides, and wanting to "go with the flow" as much as possible.

I also liked fast-forwarding into the fall and winter: same pattern of tides, but a shrinking arc of daylight, and plummeting water and air temperatures. There was the sense of things both known and unknown, of human events intersecting with celestial ones. How many more of these tides were we going to swim? That was the question that kept me flipping pages as if it were a novel.

SEPTEMBER

Labor Day was windy and only in the low seventies, and the Essex River Basin was flecked with whitecaps. Our oldest son, Jim, had brought his wife, Susan, home for the long weekend and rented a small motorboat so he could take her on a tour of the local waterways. Susan is from New Orleans, the youngest of six children in a family that has lived there for generations. They picked up Robert and me at the end of Water Street, just a short walk from where we live, and we all sped off into a blue that seemed to have shifted just slightly toward navy, a hint of the end of summer.

We hauled the boat up and stopped for lunch near Twopenny Loaf—the thumb of beach at the inland side of Wingaersheek—and afterward swam the sparkling, churning waters, though we mostly just got tossed around by a swirl of opposing currents.

Afterward, wrapped in towels, Susan and I sat on a dune and talked about the crawfish boil she was planning for us for dinner. She'd had ten pounds of the creatures FedExed from Louisiana in an insulated, gel-cooled container, and they were waiting for us in the fridge back home. They would be boiled in our twenty-gallon lobster pot, along with corn on the cob, red potatoes, andouille sausage, and a spice brew of cayenne, dill weed, paprika, clove, and coriander.

It would be a communal meal, she explained. No need to set the table except to cover it with some newspaper: After draining, we'd just dump the contents of the pot onto the middle of the table.

As we talked, I searched out the sand's warmth with my fingers and toes. The tide was creeping back in, shrinking the beaches and swallowing up the sand flats. Sailboats tacked into the wind. Cruising boats were anchored in a row along the back side of Crane Beach, a temporary neighborhood. A flotilla of kayaks headed for the beach. Gulls dove down for the flotsam of our lunch: curls of bread crust, potato chip bits. Face turned to the sun, I breathed in salt mist.

But then a Jet Ski came buzzing out of nowhere, a red-and-yellow juggernaut veering close to shore and then swerving away, a rooster tail of spray flung out behind it like fireworks.

It must have felt so perfectly, perfectly glorious to the rider.

A week later, it was dead low tide in the evening, and so it was a Conomo Point swim. As we sat on the dock, pulling on our fins and gloves, Robert noticed several

747s overhead, more large planes than usual, circling slowly like the turkey vultures that routinely scouted the marsh for carrion.

"Sometimes there are a lot of them when there's a prevailing wind in a certain direction," he said. "The air-traffic controllers send all the planes coming in from the west up our way, northeast of Logan, so they can turn around and land against the southeast wind."

It wasn't until we were back from swimming and eating dinner that we remembered it was September 11, the seventh anniversary of a day when there'd been plenty of birds in the sky but no planes, not for the rest of that day or for three days afterward. It had been an almost preternaturally beautiful late-summer day, the wrong kind of day for a disaster. Our daughter, Mary, was living a few blocks up from Ground Zero at the time; she'd just moved to Manhattan the week before. Jim worked in the Hancock Building in Boston. After we'd heard from both of them, we remembered to call David, still in high school, to let him know his siblings were okay.

I was supposed to go to my twenty-fifth high school reunion out in Southern California and had tickets for American Airlines Flight 11, Boston to L.A., a week later. I never went, partly because I couldn't imagine flying ever again, but also because the flight no longer existed. I've told this story many times to other people and heard their stories of where they were and what they were doing when they heard the news about the World Trade Center attack.

"Every one of us occupies a portion of space," Abraham Joshua Heschel wrote in *The Sabbath.* "He takes it up exclusively. The portion of space which my body occupies is taken up by myself in exclusion of anyone else. Yet no one possesses time. There is no moment which I possess exclusively. This very moment belongs to all living men as it belongs to me."

BIOLOGIST

"Swimming in them? *Really?*"

It was mid September, and I was telling a friend about Robert's and my obsession with swimming the saltwater creeks. We were having lunch at Panera, catching up.

"Not at low tide," I clarified. "At high tide, it's like this long, looping lap pool."

"Cool." Dorothy Boorse is a biology professor and textbook author whose research specialty is wetlands and invasive species. She has spoken in venues ranging from her classrooms to town halls to the halls of the U.S. Congress. But no matter where she is, she's street theater, a scientist with a wide-eyed urgency about getting people outdoors so that they're in a position to care about the places where they live, move, and where they exist. From time to time in a conversation, she will pause, tilting her head ever so slightly, scanning around for the part of the big picture that might best connect with *this* particular human.

"Edge ecologies are *so* important," she said. "Things happen there that don't happen anywhere else."

And just like that, she had found my soft spot. Maybe she'd pegged me as an edgy creature, a boundary stalker. I'd been an odd kid, drawn instinctively to any of the world's hinterlands that were available to me: the barranca that ran like a jagged gash behind our upscale subdivision in Southern California; the quiet, hot middles of lemon orchards; the outfield of softball games, where I rarely had to chase a ball, and where I could pay attention to crabgrass and anthills.

"Salt marshes are particularly rich ecotones," Dorothy was saying. "*Eco-* is from the Greek *oikos,* for 'household'; *tonos* means 'tension.' Two 'households' in a fertile sort of tension."

Because the *Spartina* species (and a few other plants) are adapted to handle twice-daily immersion in salt water, she explained, they dominate the coastal marshes. Each year, marshlands convert enormous amounts of solar energy into grass, and although few creatures directly eat the grass, as it decomposes it becomes a vast, nutrient-rich environment for bacteria, algae, and fungi. These organisms, in turn, are food for snails, shrimp, oysters, clams, and hermit crabs—and so on up the food chain to muskrats and foxes and humans.

"More than two thirds of marine fish start their lives in estuaries," she said. "They wouldn't exist without this environment as a nursery."

Even aside from its roles as feeder and protector of species, she went on, this thick peat bed was also unequaled as a kind of continental front bumper, a shock-absorbing barrier to storm surge.

"Levees and seawalls are our human attempts at the same thing, but they're nowhere near as effective as healthy marshes. Katrina, in 2005, for example. That was much more severe than it would have been if Louisiana hadn't lost so much of its wetlands."

In Louisiana, nearly two thousand square miles of wetland habitat had been lost, mostly because of human activity, to the Gulf of Mexico between 1932 and 2000. Adding insult to injury, Katrina had destroyed many more thousands of acres of wetlands after the fact. Though Louisiana was the canary in the coal mine, wetland loss there mirrored a more general loss nationwide: Only half of the nation's original salt marshes still exist.

"Here's the thing: Marshes perform 'ecosystem services' that are impossible, or at least unfathomably expensive, to re-create with technology," Dorothy said. "Plus, at least forty percent of the world's economy and eighty percent of the needs of the poor come from biological resources. With climate change and sea-level rise, we'll need these resources more than ever—but we continue to lose them. Later on, we'll wish we'd treated them better."

In nearly an hour, neither of us had made much of a dent in our salads. As we waited for containers to take our leftovers home in, she started to tell me about carbon sequestration, but she must have read something in my gaze that meant incomprehension.

"We'll talk more," she said. We both had things we needed to get back to.

I have mentioned conditions for keeping a practice going—removing obstacles, having a buddy, and so on—but my conversation with Dorothy that day provided the most important one: What you are doing needs to *matter,* to connect with your sense of the work you have been born into the world to do.

At night I burrow against Robert as he drifts off to sleep (he is usually first to go). In the early years of our relationship, when our bodies were younger and more nearly perfect, I needed to be alone—not touching Robert or being touched—when it was time to fall asleep. Now we sleep stuck together, front to back, and if we've drifted apart during the night I'll seek out some skin like a swimmer heading for land.

(A lot has happened between us over the years: intimacy, fertility, and, occasionally, alienation and a sense of the ultimate unknowability of the other. There will always be the shadow side, the places in the psyche too private or inaccessible to share.)

We dream. This is categorical: All humans do it, along with—apparently—all mammals, and some birds. I don't recall my dreams whole, but am left with a kind of afterimage, something barely perceptible and highly specific at the same time. Some of these after-images persist for years, a substrate to my life I know little about. It's just out of reach as I get out of bed and feel about with my feet and hands for the pile of clothing I wear early in the morning—dark sweatpants, dark T-shirt or turtleneck, socks, and slippers. This is my early-morning persona: fuzzy around the edges, but alert and ready for (interior) action.

Whichever of us is awake first in the morning starts the coffee. While it brews, we head in opposite directions to our studios. Mine is an attic on the third floor of our house, its large skylight facing the gable-end window of Robert's studio, which occupies the second floor of the barn adjacent to the house. The two windows stand about thirty feet apart and at about the same height from the ground. At my skylight, I can track Robert's shadow passing back and forth across the window as he paints and stands back from his work. In cold weather, the chimney shoots puffs of smoke into the early-morning sky. Painting is not his day job, as writing is not mine; we both struggle to protect a few hours each day for what we most love to do.

My laptop sits on a small table to the left of a window overlooking our front yard. The plywood subfloor, painted brown, is covered with hand-me-down rugs, and the curtain on the small window is an India-print tablecloth, too long for the window, draped over two nails.

It's a protected space and a protected time, too early in the day for the tug of other obligations. Still, each day I have to shepherd myself into getting started. I thumb through little slips of paper with scrawled notes to myself, and scroll through the previous day's work. If it's a good day, the writing catches, like an engine starting up.

Studios are not so much hermitages—fixed places for a fulltime vocation—as tabernacles, temporary shelters for devotion to something bigger and more complex than oneself. It's not just the frame itself; it's also the frame of mind it makes room for. It's a safe place for chasing down an obsession that is often intensely private. You can stop looking over your shoulder and just dive down, trusting for at least a little while in the integrity of your own story, with its tenuous connections, rabbit trails, and dead ends—and its occasional epiphanies.

It helps, of course, to live with someone who is in the same boat.

"How are your little cars and trucks?" Robert and I sometimes ask each other. This translates roughly as "How's your writing/painting/thinking going?" The metaphor comes from our oldest son who, as a preschooler, loved his Matchbox cars and trucks intensely. When he wasn't playing with them he was arranging them: in rows, in a circle around the edge of the dining table, and into categories and subcategories. He carried them around in a wicker basket and asked any willing adult: "Do you want to look at my little cars and trucks, and talk about them?"

One of us really should have had a gift for investment banking, but this is how two artists get through life: by splitting up the day-job obligations that keep food on the table, and practicing forbearance when a project stretches out for years, with no obvious payback on the horizon. This is a way of loving another person: to grant them the space and time for the pursuit of what they love.

On work mornings, I have an hour or so—sometimes more, sometimes less. It has to happen here and now or it won't happen. At exactly quarter to eight, I shower, the first ritual of leaving one world and entering another for the day. But the warm water pelting my head and back and torso extends the morning world a bit longer. I've got one eye on the clock (so easy to spend too much time in the shower) and one on the needles of water shooting from the showerhead, inches from my face. Then white steam clouds rise and fill the stall, for a few tantalizing minutes gathering up everything.

COLD

Around here (latitude: 42; longitude: -70), water temperatures drop to the mid-to-low sixties by the end of summer. Take a brisk walk in sixty-five-degree air and you'll work up a sweat. But in sixty-five-degree water, you don't warm up no matter how energetically you swim. That's because of heat transfer—the exchange of heat from a warm object to a cooler one—which happens about thirty times faster in the water than in the air. We felt this heat extraction first in our hands and feet, the parts of our bodies farthest from our hearts.

One evening we swam up Ebben Creek farther than we'd been before, where the channel narrows to the point where you can almost touch one side with your toes and the other with your fingertips. Enticed by the snort of horses in a field upriver, I wanted to keep going, ignoring the fact that we'd already come close to a mile upriver, that the tide wouldn't turn for another hour, and that we'd have to swim a long way back against the current.

About halfway back, Robert had one of his excruciating knife-in-the-thigh leg cramps, caused by many things, but in this case it was swimming against a strong current in cool water bordering on cold. Though he's not heavy and was doing everything he could to cooperate, it took me long minutes to shove him out of the water and up onto the bank. He flopped onto high ground, twitching like a fish.

After the leg cramp subsided somewhat, he was able to stand, then walk shakily. I steered him away from the ditches and holes, which seemed to have multiplied in the semidarkness.

We made a third trip to the dive store. We had thought the several thin layers we had—Farmer Johns, plus sleeveless hooded vests, plus long-sleeve wetsuit shirts— would cumulatively fend off the cold. But though these layers helped with the initial shock of entering cold water, they weren't enough to keep our core temperatures up. Robert had already gone online and researched water-temperature charts and the recommended types of suits for different gradations of cold. I'd found some instructions (italic passages below) regarding how a wetsuit should fit.

Fit is a very important aspect to consider when buying a wetsuit. If your wetsuit does not fit properly it will not be able to keep you warm or allow you the mobility you need for your sport.

Robert went first into the single dressing room, carrying several full-length "4/3" suits (four millimeters of insulation at the torso, three at the arms and legs; meant for water temperatures between sixty-three and fifty-eight degrees). I browsed the suits, wondering if we would ever need the 6/5 versions (for water approximately forty-two degrees and below). At the end of the rack were the drysuits, which looked like colorful Gore-Tex spacesuits.

A few minutes later, Robert emerged, graying chest hair sprouting from the neck of the suit, which had a nifty chartreuse thunderbolt running diagonally across the torso. He did some deep knee bends.

After you have your wetsuit on there should be no excess room, including the torso, crotch, shoulders and knees. It should fit tight in order to keep only a thin layer of water between your body and your suit.

"Hard to tell where the line is between tight and constricting," he said, reaching both arms up over his head, then touching his toes. "But I think this is about right."

My turn in the changing room.

Gently pull the fabric up and over your hips until the wetsuit is at your crotch. Make sure that the fabric around your legs is not twisted. Now pull the suit up over your torso, making sure it fits very tightly against the skin and that there is no extra fabric left along your torso before you put the arms on.

I cracked the door open, motioning for Robert. He tugged my zipper up. The neckband pressed uncomfortably against my throat.

Make sure that the neck of the wetsuit is directly against your skin. This will create a seal so just the right amount of water enters the suit. If your suit is loose, an abundance of water will flush through.

While I'd been struggling with the suit, he'd been finding boots in both our sizes, and heavier fins meant for boots instead of bare feet. The fins were split, rather than the paddle style we'd been using since the summer.

The split creates a vortex that assists in propulsion and speed. Split fins are good for casual divers, inexperienced divers who may not have good kicking technique yet, and divers who have ankle or knee problems and cramp easily.

Gloves were last. Getting the first one on was not so difficult, but putting on the second one—with no fingers free—took a while. The dressing room was too warm; our faces were flushed.

Neoprene's air-filled cells trap body heat, approximating the very dense fur of an otter and the thick blubber of a seal or whale. Fins—made of various combinations of plastic and rubber—mimic a fish's flexible fins, a duck's webbed feet. But it's still just prosthetics, unavoidably more cumbersome than the real thing—and cussedly uncomfortable on land.

It wasn't until the next evening, as we slipped into the Tilt-A-Whirl current between Conomo Point and Cross Island, that all that new snugness felt just right. We were more buoyant with our thicker neoprene skins, and, once the water inside our suits matched our respective body temperatures, we'd be warmer, too. We'd also gained more power in our legs with the new fins.

Emboldened, we swam farther than we'd been before, all the way around the western end of the island. Out of the tidal strait, the current was calm enough to pause and tread water. We'd been here many times before in boats and kayaks. But things look different when you're peering at them from sea level. When your eyes are just half a foot above water, the horizon is less than a mile away. And Cross Island—just a ten-acre blip of an island—loomed like the edge of a continent.

Many times we'd motored or paddled by the iconic summer cottage perched up on a grassy bluff. It had faded blue shingles and a wraparound front porch. This time, free of boats to anchor or stash, we decided to take a look.

Carrying our fins like satchels, we scrambled up the bluff, our new gloves and boots insulated with tepid water. Stepping onto the porch, we cupped our hands over our eyes and peered in each window, piecing together the first floor: a front room facing the bay, sheets thrown over its couch and wicker chairs; a mini-kitchen with 1960s linoleum and knotty-pine paneling; a narrow staircase leading up to the sleeping loft, its treads worn.

A grassy path led uphill from the house and disappeared into the wooded interior of the island. Our boots squished as we trod the grassy, tree-overhung path, passing an abandoned tennis court and a Shingle style house several times larger than the blue cottage.

We emerged on the island's east coast, approaching what had always been a familiar landmark out in the bay: a stone foundation that was rumored to have been the beginnings of a "spite" house. Someone in the extended family that owned the island had decided to block the view of another relative. That's what we'd heard, anyway. The unfinished foundation stood at the edge of the island like a question mark.

Somewhere during our trek across the island, the tide had turned. We'd swum against the current on the way and would be swimming against it on the way back if we retraced our path. Instead, we walked across the exposed mudflat that edges the east side of the island, reentering the channel upriver.

Back at the dock, we'd come full circle. But we'd also traced a widening arc.

Anywhere you are, things scale up and out. The whirlpool in the middle of a tidal strait is a baby version of deep-ocean maelstroms. The footpath across a ten-acre island is cousin to the transcontinental highway. Family feuds over sight lines scale up to global warfare.

Things scale down and inward, too. Cross Island is actually not a monolithic island; it's one of three oak islands perched on a slab of salt marsh out in the middle of Essex Bay. The other two, Corn and Dilly, are mere fractions of an acre. All around them are mini-islands too numerous to count, with names that exist only in the minds of birds.

A few days later, I arrived home from work grumpy, a spat with a colleague nagging at me. I felt she had been in the wrong, but I also didn't want to be wrong and not know it.

"Why don't we go swimming?" Robert asked.

"It's late," I said.

He stretched his arm toward the western sky, fingers parallel with the horizon, and squinted. "So? We still have two and a half hours of daylight left." (Along with measuring the hours till sunset with his fingers, he also measures distances with his stride, or, in the case of a thunderclap, with his ear—each five-second lapse between the lightning flash and the cracking sound means one mile away.)

And that was how we ended up on the Clammer's Beach side of Conomo Point, at the juncture of the Essex River and Walker Creek, hoping to swim Walker Creek all the way down to the Concord Street bridge. The swimmable part of the creek was a hundred-some feet from shore, across a shimmering mudflat. Carrying our fins, we followed the path of generations of clammers, who had fortified this first bit of muddy shore with gravel and crushed clamshells, creating a ramp for the entry and exit of their motorboats.

Reaching the end of that semisolid ground, we started off across the mud, alert to subtle differences in texture that marked varying degrees of firmness in the chocolate-colored mud of the creek bottom. "Pluff" mud can be as enveloping as quicksand. If you lose a sneaker, it may be gone for good.

We slid into the chute of water hugging the far side of the creek and swam hard against the current. The ends of ditches and natural canals punctuated the mud walls, curving enticingly inward. All quiet except for the rhythmic plinking of our hands stroking and fins kicking, and the occasional caw of a gull overhead. Ahead of us, on the more solid, inhabited side of the creek, three docks jutted out, a cabin cruiser tied up at one of them.

An invisible someone was talking, the voice indistinct at first, then louder. As we swam closer, a tiny figure appeared from behind the boat, hands up around his head.

"There's a house under construction," Robert remarked. "Maybe it's the contractor on his cell phone." But as we swam closer, the shouting turned into oratory. The figure was a teenage boy in a hoodie, pacing restlessly out on a long dock—an actor on a stage he must have thought was utterly private. We swam by, keeping a low profile.

Around the next bend in the creek, the swimmable chute got wider and shallower. Soon we were not so much swimming as mud-skating, in water that was just over a foot deep. The motion was something like cross-country skiing, but instead of kick and glide, it was extend an arm, plunge fingers into mud, pull, then repeat with opposite arm. Tiny fish nipped at my wetsuit.

The water got shallower and shallower, and finally we had to stand up.

"I guess we'll swim to the bridge another time," I said. The creek bottom in the middle of the channel was sandy, though, firm enough for us to walk a ways—fins off—before turning back.

"That's Jan Smith's boathouse," Robert said, pointing out a small shed tucked into the eastern side of the creek. On the western shore stood the large, solidly built dock that had belonged to the Cohens, a real estate magnate and his artist wife. Every year, at the beginning of August, they'd hosted "end of the greenhead season" parties (greenheads are vicious biting flies that plague the area for a few weeks in July). Next to the Cohen's I could just make out Helen Tory's studio. Her métier is the monoprint. I'd visited her studio, had admired the images of goats and sheep and sumo wrestlers, but had never had this view of her world.

Robert pointed out a canal leading to the shore near Helen's studio. It had been dug years ago, probably to allow boat access to the marsh during low tide, probably by a particular reclusive fisherman who had lived nearby.

"He really *knew* fish," Robert said. "He knew exactly

when and where they came to feed. He'd only fish at night because he didn't want people following him."

As the creek narrowed, its shores grew denser and denser with the lives and stories of our neighbors.

FALL EQUINOX

Early to mid October in New England can range from freak snowstorms to days that feel like summer, and it was on one of these incongruously warm days—fall colors, summer temperatures—that we swam Ebben Creek on a Sunday afternoon. The Farnham's parking lot was full as we slipped into the water.

It was also the last of several days of new-moon tides; only the top half foot of the grass lining the channels was still showing. Our sense of scale shifted as we swam over the channels rather than down in them, over a marsh lawn that seemed laminated. We swam past cedar saplings and bushes that were not normally underwater, past small, temporary islands where birds stood in the rising tide like sentries.

About a mile upriver, we sat on a bit of submerged bank before turning back, water up to our waists, our legs more floating than dangling, wanting to extend what was probably going to be our last summer-temperature swim for the year.

It had become a game for me to try to pinpoint the turning of the tide, but millions of cubic feet of water in a tidal channel do not change direction neatly. There are many strata of water, many places where the water is slowed down by a bottleneck, and so the pivot happens in many places, in fits and starts.

We watched the glassy plane of water begin, ever so slightly, to drop. As we floated back with the current, more of the grass emerged, the outlines of the channels gradually coming clear again.

A few days later, it was blustery and a full twenty degrees colder. The water temperature had dropped to fifty, after several weeks of hovering in the mid-fifties. We swam Conomo Point in a silver-and-blue chop that slapped our faces and kept them wet. I'd worn three-fingered gloves, and as my hands began to stiffen, I squeezed my entire hand into the middle pocket, instead of just my middle and ring fingers, hoping all five digits would keep one another warm, but no.

Back at the car, I had to guide one hand with the other to get the key in the ignition. At home, we made a beeline for our outdoor hot tub, peeling off our suits, gloves, and boots, washing off as quickly as possible with the garden hose. We climbed in gingerly, our chilled skin stinging as it hit the water. A few minutes later came the reward: bathtub warmth, even as the wind picked up, sending a cottony, dark gray storm cloud from the west and, with it, little pinpricks of mist. Only Robert's head was above water, the rest of him refracted at an impossible angle beneath the water.

I slid down so the water was right at my chin, and watched droplets of mist dissolve in the steam. Then a teeny hailstone landed on my nose.

By the third week of October, New England salt-marsh lawns have turned uniformly yellow. We swam Ebben Creek, and made our way through stuff that had been flushed out of the marsh's nooks and corners: sticks, logs, a deflated, sun-bleached Mylar balloon, and broken-up bits of pumpkin. Most of all, though, we swam through flecks and clumps and barges of hay. Curious, I plowed into one of these barges rather than dodging it. It parted as I swam through. It felt like a soggy though buoyant sleeping bag.

Swimming with hay is a little eccentric. But there's nothing dirty here, if by "dirty" you mean foul or filthy or dangerous to human health. It's just cellulose—nice, clean organic matter.

For many of the years of our marriage, I had worked with another form of cellulose. Walker Creek Furniture, our family's custom furniture business, was all about wood, and about tradition. "We use mortise-and-tenon joinery instead of dowels," our website stated, "and smooth our boards with a hand plane rather than a belt sander. While most furniture is finished with a sprayed-on polyurethane or colored lacquer, we finish every piece by hand using linseed oil, shellac and milk paint."

I learned to "read" wood grains as I sanded and oiled and polished the surfaces of tables and cabinets and chairs. I was intimately acquainted with the types of wood most commonly used in furniture making: pine, hemlock, ash, cherry, maple, mahogany, oak, and walnut. Pine and other softwoods grow quickly; their grains are loose, with lots of space between growth rings. The hardwoods grow more slowly, resulting in denser, more luxurious-looking grains. Bird's-eye maple and figured birch would shift with the light, flaming out as you walked around them.

I also became close friends with the substances we put *on* wood. Milk paint, for example, was a mix of casein (milk solids), limestone, clay, and earth pigments. We used a commercially available version of the paint, which involved mixing the powder with hot water and stirring it with a wire whisk to eliminate lumps. After applying the paint and letting it dry, we sanded the surface with progressively finer grits of sandpaper, then polished it with extra-fine ("quadruple-aught") steel wool. The result was a durable, nontoxic finish as smooth as marble. Sometimes I spent all day with a single color, contemplating it with my hands as well as with my eyes. These were the colors of the marshes and the woods: the umber of mud, the celadons of lichen, the red oxide of a rusting barrel stave, the whites of chalk or lime.

When I used milk paint, or other simple substances, like linseed oil and shellac, I knew where they came from. Linseed oil comes from the dried, ripened seeds of the flax plant. When used on wood, it produces a shiny but not overly glossy surface that highlights the grain of the wood. Shellac is a resin secreted by the female lac bug. It functions as natural primer and high-gloss varnish.

We also used contemporary paints, stains, and solvents. Nearly all of these were derived from another common earth material: petroleum—literally "rock oil"—that had been pressed and cooked underground for millions of years. But the connection between crude oil and these refined substances was harder to grasp. It involved a long line of inventive people who had, beginning in the late nineteenth century, engineered these substances into everything from paint thinners to paintbrushes. Much of this engineering took place at a molecular, invisible level.

The downside of petroleum distillates' shape-shifting ingenuity is the long list of things that can happen—to you or your surroundings—if you handle them carelessly. Rags saturated with oil and crumpled up in a trash bag can self-ignite (we knew someone whose house had burned to the ground this way). Spray paints and lacquers contain volatile organic compounds (VOCs) like acetone, xylene, toluene, and benzene, which can irritate your skin and eyes, mess with your central nervous system, or—worst-case-scenario—trigger a chain reaction of disruptions in the red blood cell–forming capacity of your bone marrow. There is, in short, usually a direct connection between the complexity of a product and its potential for collateral damage.

NOVEMBER

On the last day of daylight saving time, we swam Conomo Point as the tide neared high. The wooden floats attached to the stone dock had been removed and stored for the season, so by then we were entering the water from the flat rocks projecting into the channel.

We swam toward the year's last 5:30 sunset. Salmon and magenta clouds clustered at the horizon as the sun, a gold lozenge, slid down, disappearing below the tree line of a distant shore in Ipswich. A few minutes later, the sky exploded into at least six distinct colors. Floating on our backs, we counted and named them: pale gray, gunmetal gray, jet-trail white, sheep's wool white, baby blue, turquoise. Then the finale: gold flung out everywhere, the unseen sun gilding the undersides of every cloud.

Over the next quarter hour, the color drained from the clouds. We treaded water awhile near the tip of Cross Island before heading back.

"It's just turned," Robert said, meaning the tide.

"How can you tell?"

He pointed to a Boston Whaler, one of the few

boats still moored in the channel. Sure enough, it had done a 180 while I wasn't watching, and was now pointed east. I often looked for the turning of the tide but seldom saw it, the exact moment as elusive as the moment of falling asleep.

Later that evening, we were up in Robert's painting studio, an attic dense with stuff and with possibilities.

"That felt like the end," I said. "Not the end of swimming, but the end of swimming at night."

"Why?" Robert asked. He was feeding the fire in the woodstove, adding a log and blowing on the coals to get it to catch. I was sprawled on the couch, a comfortable castoff from a friend's house, its blue upholstery sun-bleached. *The Köln Concert* played softly on an ancient stereo.

"Because it'll be dark tomorrow."

"There's nothing in the water after dark that isn't there before dark," Robert said, reasonably enough.

"This is true," I replied, meaning, *Yes, that is factually correct, but it doesn't change how I feel about it.*

"It's been getting dark while we're swimming for a while now," he said.

"That's true, too." But getting into the water while it was still at least marginally light was a kind of on-ramp for me, sliding me past resistance. Tomorrow, that on-ramp would be gone.

The next evening, we drove to the Point at our usual time, but now 5:30 was an hour past sunset. The moon was in its first quarter, with Mars and Venus up in the west. There was still a slight glow above the horizon. The water was navy blue ink, spangled with moonlight.

Crouched on a flat rock jutting out into the channel, fins tucked under my right arm, I wavered. But seconds after Robert shot into the current, I leaped into the water, rolling over briefly to pull on my fins, then angling my body toward Robert's so we could cross the channel more or less together. All I could see of him was the flash of moonlight on his head. I swam toward that flash, grasped the hump of neoprene that was his left shoulder.

No boats coming in either direction for as far as we could see. We swam hard through the choppy middle of the chute between the Point and Cross Island, then reached the calmer current on the other side. We floated toward the western tip of the island in longitudinal stripes of moonlight.

I had thought of dark as a kind of monolith, but it was an environment rich in sensory cues. Above the surface, these cues took the form of light, giving you detailed information about the shape of the water: its ropes of current, its bucklings and disruptions. I could still see the water, but I was viewing it through a different filter.

Below the surface, proprioception took over. Each extension or contraction of any muscle in my body was noted by my muscle spindles, the specialized cells in each muscle bundle that tracked the shifting lengths of these bundles and conveyed the information to my central nervous system.

The result was a richly detailed nonvisual map of where my body was in relation to an ever-shifting matrix of space and time.

After the switch back to standard time, I began logging our swims. It was several weeks past the date we had thought it would all be over, and I wanted to keep track of the final leg of the journey. We'd already agreed that it was not going to be a stunt; we would keep swimming only as long as we were still enjoying it. I noted the basics: location, weather, time of day or night, what the sky and water looked like, other creatures we saw, and what they were up to.

By this time we were swimming mostly in the evenings after work, with an occasional daytime swim. I sometimes jotted down what we thought and talked about as we swam, or on the way home, or over dinner afterward. Sometimes the entries turned into essays, in the older sense of an *assay,* an attempt.

We had made yet another trip to the dive store, buying the "6/5" suits that had seemed so unlikely back in the summer, along with boots and gloves with ankle and wrist seals—basically a drysuit for the extremities.

11/4—Ebben Creek, air 60°, water 47°. Quick swim after work, all the way dark by the end; the yellow Farnham's sign welcomed us home.

11/5—Ebben Creek, air 59°, water 50°. In at 4:15, out by 5:00. Still light for a while, but since it was cloudy, it was a very filtered light, with soft, saturated color fields: abalone water, yellow-orange grass. The colors drained as the sky darkened, everything turning to gray scale. Half-moon going in and out of clouds. The fog thickened as we swam.

11/7—Ebben Creek, air 59°, water 54°. In at 5:00, out at 6:40. The moon was in its second quarter and it was about as dark as it ever gets—black water, charcoal sky, with a faint haze of ambient light to the south, in the general direction of Boston. One of the best swims we've ever had; we went a long way.

11/10—Ebben Creek, air 58°, water 54°. Unseasonably mild, so we swam with the tide nearly all the way to Grove Street. In at 5:30, out at 7:00. We swam to the second bend in the creek, where the two Adirondack chairs were still strung between a willow and an ash; the hammock had long since been put away for the winter. I waited for the tide to pause, floating upright, the tips of my fins barely brushing the bouldered bottom of the creek. Robert floated on his

back, arms and legs splayed like a starfish. Our typical stances in water were revelatory of who we are:
his trusting nature, my need to be on top of things
and know exactly where I am going at all times.

11/11—Ebben Creek, air 49°, water 47°. We had the day
off and swam the creek at noon. Maybe because we
were hungry, the conversation turned to oysters—
specifically the eastern oyster, *Crassostrea virginica*.
"There used to be so many oysters here that the
bottoms of the creeks weren't muddy," Robert said,
floating on his back, free-associating. "Or so I've
heard. Bob Parlee—Bob over on Milk Street? His
wife was one of Mary's teachers?—tried to get an
oyster farm going over near Songinese Creek. I don't
know how that turned out." Pause. "Do you know
why their shells are so bumpy?" Another pause.
"They take on whatever shape they're attached to,
usually something bumpy or rocky."

We didn't find any oysters, but we did see
ribbed mussels (*Geukensia demissa*) tucked away
in the creek walls, where they attach themselves to
cordgrass roots (unlike their close cousin, the blue
mussel, which attaches to pilings or rocks). Similar
in shape and size to the blue mussel, they're yel-
lowish brown to brownish black, with corrugated
ribs running the length of the shell. Years ago,
kayaking one of the creeks, we'd noticed ribbed
mussels for the first time, and brought some home

and steamed them. The meat was disappointingly watery and loose, no competition for blue mussels or soft-shell clams.

There's a literary term for when something barely noticed or overly familiar emerges from the background and becomes wondrously strange and new: foregrounding. That day, bivalves came popping out of the background and were everywhere, like Waldo: sunk in the soft mud of the creek bottom, lodged in the tough roots of the cordgrass, clinging to the rocky shores farther out in the Essex River Basin. And rightly so: Bivalves and other shellfish often make up the greatest proportion of animal biomass in tidal ecosystems.

But the noun *mass* implies inertness—it is derived from the Old French *masse*: "lump, heap, pile"; Latin *massa*: "kneaded dough, lump, that which adheres together like dough." It's important to see the actions of this mass, its verbs. Bivalves aggregate; they reticulate. They send out strong, flexible threads and lash themselves together in floating condos. They become food for creatures above them on the "org chart"—the food chain—and supply habitat space for creatures below them. In their filter feeding, bivalves also remove contaminants from the waterways, improving the water habitat for other organisms. And so on. The takeaway: Biomass *is* mass—"adhering together like dough"—yet it does its own kneading, to the benefit of the greater ecosystem.

11/12—Conomo Point, air 33°, water 46°. A sudden drop in air temperature, but the water was still relatively warm. We decided to go for it, plunging into the buckling dark of the channel. Swimming around the western tip of Cross Island, we saw, for the first time, what looked like a barge. Closer, though, it turned out to be a fishing boat.

Clammers' motorboats mostly go home with their owners each night. The pleasure boats that had crowded the Point had been taken out weeks ago, now shrink-wrapped and hibernating in marinas. This boat was an outlier, like us, the crazy swimmers.

We didn't last long; we'd gotten in the water at about 5:30 and were back in the car, shivering, by a little after 6:00. Hot tub: oh *yes*.

11/13—Slight fever, no swim. I spent the evening curled up on the couch under a blanket, remembering things long past, like Ivan Muise's gas station on the Essex causeway. (Somewhere back in the late '70s/early '80s, as he and I waited for my tank to fill, Ivan had excitedly pointed out seals in the Essex River, their dog faces bobbing around the boats and moorings. "That's unusual," he said; "they don't normally come this far upriver. You see them more often at Black Rock, near Coles Island." Right at that moment, I'd seen one flip and float on its back.)

I asked Robert why he floated on his back so much. "That's what makes it like flying," he said. Sensing my incomprehension, he added, "When you tip your head back, you see the horizon not as a line but as a circle. Like cats, which seem to orient themselves upside down." (All clear now?)

11/14—Ebben Creek, air 59°, water 49°; in just before 11:00, out by 12:15. This was the first of several days of "king tides," the semiannual twelve-foot high tides that transform estuaries into temporary bays. I'd been looking forward to this for weeks. I finagled several hours off work, drove home in the middle of the day, and squeezed into my wetsuit. I'd left it hanging over a door, where it would heat up in the sun.

The box culvert under the bridge had been entirely flooded; the waterline was inching up concrete that had eroded to a coarse graininess. Thousands of tides had flowed in and out of this narrow opening since the bridge had been built, a few of them even reaching the date marker near the top of the bridge: 1934, in the font of the times.

Instead of entering Ebben Creek from the rocky platform below the bridge, I slid in just below the guardrails. My sense of scale shifted as I swam over the marsh lawn, and over the channels rather than down in them, floating over a school of minnows suspended between my body and the murky depths of the creek. I swam past small, temporary islands where herons stood and fished from currents they knew all about. The red-tailed hawk was in its usual perch in the uppermost branches of the oak tree at the first bend, but the bends were gone.

I tried to avoid shallow spots, places where I had to semicrawl, poling myself along by gripping the grass. In less of a deluge, I could still have read the channels by following the winding path of tips of grass and the flow of water. But now the currents flowed everywhere, and the water's surface was textured by wind currents that had nothing to do with the tides.

In a tide this high, stuff gets flushed out of places where it's been lodged for weeks, or months. I spotted something small and rectangular floating up ahead in the grass. I swam toward it, approaching what turned out to be a toy-size wooden barge carrying one passenger: a plastic toy soldier glued to the platform, an avatar in a vast, roiling sea.

11/15—Ebben Creek, another over-twelve-foot tide, and still unseasonably mild: air 60°, water 54°. This time I was trying to stay in the channels; scooting myself over very shallow areas the day before had left my elbows and wrists sore. Back at Farnham's, I floated near the mouth of the bridge, waiting for the creek to slow down to a quivering stillness.

11/16—Along with a sudden upswing in air temperature, it was the highest tide of the year: twelve feet, six inches, which meant even the tips of the grass were underwater. We swam a long way: By the Tidelog, high tide was supposed to be at 11:17, but in the creeks it can vary by as much as forty-five minutes, for complex weather- and hydrology-related reasons. We were trying to swim from Farnham's to just above Grove Street with the tide still coming in, then back the same way, also with the tide in our favor.

11/17—Conomo Point, air 35°, water 46°. In at 5:25, out by 6:10. We swam around the island past the blue house into the next little cove, pausing at a houseboat belonging to friends; it had been boarded up for the winter. We hung on to its dock for a few minutes, floating in black water, the current flowing around us in streaky silver curls and ripples. Shaping up to be a starry, starry night.

"Cold is relative," Robert said afterward, as we peeled off first our gloves and boots, then our suits, rinsing them off in the shower, filling its basin with little flecks of straw and seaweed. "I was as cold at certain times in August as I am at certain times now."

Temperature was out of our control, but we could manipulate other variables. That would affect—somewhat—how we experienced the cold. We ran up and down stairs to get our heart rates up before even putting on our suits. We kept in mind that the initial shock of cold water shooting down the spine was fleeting. We pushed off against a dock or a boulder, and swam right past that shock. Perhaps most important, we tried to remember to quit while we were ahead, turning back before we started really feeling the cold. Resiliency can turn on a dime.

11/19—Ebben Creek, air 28°, water 38°; ice on the marsh like cake frosting. We lasted only twenty minutes. Afterward, thawing out in the hot tub, hands and feet stinging, we wondered if we'd still be doing this at Thanksgiving.

WINTER SOLSTICE

After months of tilting farther and farther away from the sun, at the winter solstice the Earth begins its long journey back toward spring. There is no absolute pause—just as there is no actual hiatus at the top of the tide. But it's deeply ingrained in humans to seek out a still point in a spinning world.

As we swam closer and closer to this still point, cold was a constant presence that had to be managed and appeased. We'd heard about divers consuming lots of water before a dive and then periodically peeing in their suits to keep warm. We did them one better: Just before entering the water, we took turns pouring the contents of a gallon milk jug full of nearly hot water into each other's suits, then pulling up the zippers and tamping down the Velcro neck tabs.

The first infusion of seawater would turn the water inside our suits gradually lukewarm. It was not toasty, exactly, and we instinctively adopted more defensive postures in the water, not sprawling on our backs as we had earlier in the year. But this relative warmth made swimming possible in water now mostly in the low forties.

Bodily limitations held at bay, we had the privilege—unlike most other humans for most of history, unlike the other creatures around us (the muskrats and otters and minnows)—of focusing on things that were not purely necessary for survival.

11/22—Air temp has dropped into the 20s. No swim.

11/27—Walker Creek, and the gift of an unseasonably warm Thanksgiving Day: air 40°, water 46°. Mary took photos of us disappearing under the bridge and emerging on the other side, both of us looking vaguely astonished.

12/1—Walker Creek, air high 40s, water 42°. In at 11:30, out at just past noon. We swam in pewter-colored water toward the sun, which barely cleared the treetops above Great Ledge. On the return trip, the water was battleship gray in the backlighting. Then fog rolled in from the west like a blanket unfurling.

12/2—Conomo Point, air 40°, water 42°. Overhead, Venus, Jupiter, and the moon formed a tight triangle. We entered the channel at about 5:30, pausing before heading across, unsure which way we'd go. But the current decided, carrying us to the eastern side of the island, where we ran aground on a large field of seaweed-covered granite. Robert had worn a headlamp, and he pointed it downward on tiny surprised fish. Up above, the triangle had finally merged, but not really: The moon was 240,000 miles away; Venus, 3 million; and Jupiter, 359 million. (Put differently, if you were traveling at the speed of light, you'd reach the moon in two seconds, Venus in thirty seconds, and Jupiter in about nine minutes.)

12/7—Conomo Point, air 32°, water 40°. From the water we saw Christmas lights strung on trees and houses. One house had been strung with particular care: windows and corner boards and roofline, the lights obliterating the pith of the house itself, leaving only geometry.

12/12—Conomo Point, air 28°, water 40°. About two hours from low tide, and a very strong current along Cross Island. I felt a sudden loss of power in my left leg, and it took a few seconds of kicking with no traction to realize I'd lost a fin; I'd apparently not strapped it tightly enough onto my boot. Robert said afterward that he'd felt something bump up against him briefly and, recoiling, he let it pass, thinking it was a fish. Drat. (The following evening, we drove back to the dive shop, our fifth trip, to buy another pair of fins.)

12/25—Conomo Point, air low 40s, water 39°. On the way across the channel, the whirlpool in the center had a glassy, polished look, like obsidian. I swam through the paradox of smooth surface/underlying tension, the turbulence pushing and pulling me in several directions at once. Back home: a turkey in the oven, and the centripetal forces of family, food, and ritual.

12/28—Five-Family Point, air in the 50s, water in the 40s. In by a little after 3:00, out by 4:30. We crossed the channel and swam along the sandbar. Herring gulls perched several feet above us on the sandbar's continental edge. Cornflower blue sky and mackerel clouds.

12/31—Ebben Creek, an afternoon swim. Water 39°, air 29°: the coldest conditions yet, but building up to it gradually since the summer made it thinkable. Our feet broke up icy edges as we stepped into slushy water. As I pushed off, the cold surrounded me with a force I hadn't felt before. The warm water inside our suits would stay that way only for a little longer. We lasted possibly ten minutes before turning back toward the friendly glow of the yellow Farnham's sign.

On the drive home, we cranked the heat all the way up, and discussed revising our exit strategy for colder weather. We could bring along wool gloves to warm up our hands, Robert suggested. We could drive the minivan instead of the Camry, I said. We could cover the windows and change out of our wetsuits in the back *before* driving home.

I skipped the outdoor shower and went straight inside, leaving wet footprints on the kitchen floor and all the way upstairs to the bathroom. Because the boots were zipperless, it was always a bit of a struggle to peel them off. It was far easier tugging at them while sitting in a few inches of warm water in the tub and shower enclosure than outdoors with the wind blowing. Caring for a wetsuit involves rinsing off the outside, then turning it inside out and rinsing the inside, as well. I did the whole routine under pelting warm water, then hung the suit over the showerhead, awaiting the next swim.

We spent the last few hours of the year at a party. At one point, we sat in a circle and played a word game, Pass the Bomb, that involved a ticking plastic bomb. When it was your turn to hold the bomb, you picked out a card, which had several letters printed on it. You had to shout out a word that contained those letters, and pass the ticking bomb to the next player. The idea was not to be stuck holding the bomb when it exploded. I became very competitive.

When we got home I was still wide awake. While Robert drifted off, I checked my email, because you never know; there might be something important.

And there was. First, a message from our younger son, David, who was in his second year of music college. Toward the end of the message he had written: "I am learning how to look at sound waves and gHz in my music tech class and learning what visible sound is and seeing it as waves and applying it to all the music programs they have me learning. I've been thinking about how all music is composed of 12 tones. Just 12 tones. A doorbell interval is one-sixth of all music ever composed. That seems astounding to me."

And then there was the latest post in an ongoing debate with several friends about the perils and promises of cyberspace. Our friend Bruce Herman had the last word of the year on the topic: "One muddled thought to offer: all our works are subject to the laws of gravity and thermodynamics—but also hold the possibility of Glory. Anything we put our hand to is either a potential Golden Calf or a potential Holy of Holies. We and all our works will be tested by fire—and some of it presumably will not only survive the fire but be translated into that better work of a better country. May our coming year(s) shine in the midst of the almost certain falling of empire."

JANUARY

On New Year's Day, temperatures plunged to the high single digits, and the creek's edges grew a thick cuticle of ice. It was still technically possible to swim—seawater freezes at 28.4°F—but we'd already agreed there would be no stunts, no doing it just so we could say we had.

A few days later, instead of swimming, we walked through the woods in a snowstorm, tracing a path between our back door and Ebben Creek. This involved several minor breaches of private property. First, we cut across the driveway of a condo development. Then we ducked around a gate and crept into the unfenced back side of the mini–storage complex that abuts the condos. A snowplow emerged around a corner and paused. The driver peered out at us.

"Just out for a walk," Robert said, and that seemed to satisfy Snowplow Man, who shrugged and kept going. (Afterward, Robert said he'd been tempted to put on his best Obi-Wan stare and intone, "These aren't the droids you're looking for.")

We scrambled up the unfenced hill behind the mini–storage complex into woods, mostly second-growth cedar and white pine. A few years earlier, Robert had blazed a path through here down to the creek, but he was having a hard time finding it again. Fallen trees, a new fence at the edge of a construction project, a pile of asphalt blocks—all of these can obscure an old path. And snow is the great leveler; it was already half a foot deep and falling fast.

"I'm so disoriented," Robert said, something I rarely hear him say. But after a few minutes of bushwhacking, we came to a stone wall, and he knew instantly right where we were. The wall runs from just above Farnham's and continues in pretty much a straight shot toward Grove Street. These walls are everywhere in the Cape Ann woods. Eighteenth-century farmers had to cut down trees and then clear their land of boulders, and it made sense to use the stone for boundary walls. This wall now has little to do with land divisions, but much of it is still standing.

We trudged through powdery snow into clearer underbrush-free woods, and a different cohort of trees: mostly hickory and black locust, oak and maple. The ground sloped down more sharply toward sea level, and with it the bright horizontal slash between trees that meant the marsh was just ahead. We ducked under branches and there we were, about fifty feet from the second bend in the creek, the two Adirondack chairs up on the bank now covered with snow. Our parka hoods up and zipped, we approached the water, careful of snow-covered ditches. The edges were slushy, tinged yellow with hay detritus. In the middle of the channel, black water ran freely, dotted with snowflakes.

We stood there at the edge of the creek in hooded tunnel vision, in the protective intimacy of sharing an unusual obsession. This was only minimally about finding a footpath down to the creek, especially when the path traced a circuitous route behind retail businesses and through a patchwork of property boundaries, and was far less convenient than just taking the road.

But what you see from the road is one kind of truth about a place. Route 133 is the story of enterprise and boundaries and legal, agreed-upon pathways through the land. What you see from inside this thirty-acre triangle of land—bounded by the creek on the east, by the mini–storage complex to the north, and Grove Street to the south—is ground truth, a term used to refer to information provided by direct observation. With shifts in elevation, you see different kinds of vegetation; you trace out the gradual transition from woodland to marsh edge to creek. One minute you are on land that is in the middle of being shaped into something else; the next moment you are back in a place that is just biding its time.

Five years from now, we will probably not be able to take this walk. It takes only one chain-link fence, one sternly

worded sign (PREMISES PROTECTED BY . . .) to block off
an entire path. Over the past forty years, property values
in Essex County, especially along the coast, have swelled
up like bread dough. (We built our first house in 1979
for about thirty thousand dollars, half of which was for
five acres of land.) Land that sold back then for a few
thousand dollars an acre is now prime real estate, and
I can't blame anyone for selling their acreage for much
more than they paid for it. It means a comfortable retirement, and something to pass on to your children. At
the same time, I'm grateful for the people who had the
means to donate property to Essex County Greenbelt or
the Trustees of Reservations: the Stavroses and Coxes
and Bents, the Cranes and Warrens and Welds.

A hundred years from now, if predictions about a
sea-level rise of forty inches come to pass, Ebben Creek
may no longer have its grassy buffer between water and
uplands. Along with the nine other creeks branching
off from the Essex River, it could become an inlet of
the Essex Bay, its waters covering the marsh and lap-
ping against the slope into the uplands. It will look the
way it now does at an especially high tide. Farnham's
and the old Burnham house—any building currently
at sea level—will either be gone or up on stilts, and the
small bridge over the creek will have been replaced by
a higher, longer span.

It will be left to archaeologists of the future to sift
through the remains of our culture, to make a guess

about what life was like here in this postmodern, postindustrial blip of time. But, notes one professor of archaeology:

> The further into the future we go, the more likely it becomes that our *unintended* material remains will be the ones to survive. . . . Archaeologists of the yet more distant future, two, three, or four thousand years away, may find themselves reconstructing the flesh of our material world—paper, plastics, wood—based only on surviving ceramics, the odd fossil, and certain stable metals or alloys: just as we today attempt to reconstruct the wooden hafts of stone tools, or the architecture of ancient houses based only on the holes into which supporting posts were fitted. . . . Stone, of course, is the ultimate chemically resistant material.

Archaeologists will uncover stone walls, concrete slabs and basements, bridge foundations, roadbeds. The houses in this neighborhood will all seem very close together, and it may not be obvious that these were peculiar times, when it was possible to ignore your nearest neighbors because your real tribes were elsewhere.

SWIMMING IN PARENTHESES

Tuning my breath to the rhythm of peak and ebb: inhale on the rise, exhale on the fall. (As a kid in pools, I hopped more than swam.) Here it's pool-shallow blue a long way out, then the crisp transition to navy, then the bank of periwinkle clouds at the horizon. I'm out beyond the surf zone, where waves swell but don't break. Air bubbles sizzle as they break against the beach. The sand is pinhead-size orbs of calcium carbonate.

I climb up onto the breakwater to look at tidepools: chitons embedded in the rock; black urchins showing a little red when they open up; an electric-blue anemone in the depths.

I am 1,245 miles from home, in Nassau, the capital and largest city of the Bahamas.

Five women in a time-share kitchen fixing breakfast. Mine is grits with yogurt and raisins. The time-share, Harborside, is on Paradise Island, and is part of the Atlantis complex of hotels, pools, casino, and water park. We walk to the beach together, passing lizards sunning on retaining walls, and the harbor, with its slips for pleasure boats the size of small cruise ships. Sleek, towering vessels with clubhouses, dimly glimpsed bars, and large-screen TVs (the previous night we'd passed a singer out on deck, crooning a love song to what appeared to be an empty boat).

The Rapids River, a mile-long winding chute of terra-cotta concrete, is engineered to keep tube-riding human bodies flowing without getting banged up. Its sinuous path connects all the pools and water-slide attractions, which include the Abyss, the Surge, the Drop, the Serpent Slide, and the Leap of Faith, a sixty-foot, almost-vertical drop from the pinnacle of a repro-duction of a Mayan temple.

We float in blue tubes, from time to time staying together by hanging on to one another's feet or tube han-dles. The gentle rocking motion, the lukewarm water: "This is the best Tuesday I've had in years," Janet says. Then a PerfectSwell wave surge splits us apart.

You must pass through a casino to get to Aquaven-ture, wandering to the beat of seven hundred different slot-machine sound tracks. It all adds up to something like C major seventh, which tends to convey happiness and confidence. And that orange-tentacled fireball sus-pended from the casino ceiling? That's Dale Chihuly's blown-glass *Temple of the Sun*.

Back at Harborside, the evening news is on: Rocket

attacks in Gaza. The collapse of the Icelandic banking system. Bank of America getting sued over its Internet Ponzi scheme. The soaring rate of home foreclosures. More story hooks float by on the news ticker at the bottom of the screen: TODDLER BORN WITH A FOOT IN HIS BRAIN HAILED AS MIRACLE BABY.

I'm not acclimated to this. Robert and I haven't had a functioning TV in years. We have a paper subscription to *The New York Times* and a digital subscription to *The Washington Post,* where you can control the pacing of information. In our young-adult years, that pacing was even slower. We got our news first thing in the morning with birdsong, classical music, and then the "subterranean tones and pregnant pauses" of the Boston-based radio host Robert J. Lurtsema, who, it was reported in his obituary, threatened to quit when NPR wanted to insert its own news segments into *Morning Pro Musica.*

"I don't think there's anything wrong with a quiet spot once in a while," Lurtsema was quoted as saying. "When I pause I'm visualizing my audience, the person I'm speaking to. I always imagine I'm speaking to someone in particular."

Snorkeling in the lagoon the next day, I've drifted under the floating safety line to an in-between part of the water park, where a vast bloom of cauliflowerlike jellyfish carpet the lagoon floor. Each jellyfish dome is divided up, pielike, into eight florets, each floret with many tonguelike protuberances ranging in color from olive green to royal purple. I float in this forbidden area, rapt, until I am finally tweeted out by a lifeguard.

Back onshore, my friends are bundled up in blue-and-white-striped towels. The sun passes in and out of clouds, and there's a stiffening breeze. Someone has left two fresh towels on my chair. I cover up as much of my body as I can, settle down, and pick up my e-reader. We all have them now. Five devices, five portals leading to five different places.

Mine opens up into the icy labyrinth of the Canadian archipelago, where, in 1845, the Franklin expedition's ice-breaking ships attempted to forge a trade route linking the Atlantic to the Pacific. I already know it will not end well. The expedition will be locked in ice for two winters in Victoria Strait. The crew members who attempt to travel south on foot will carry many items not needed in the Arctic, and will lack many of the tools, strategies, and attitudes that actually could have helped them survive.

The Inuit people of the Canadian Northeast, on the other hand, had survived the severe Arctic climate for centuries. The Franklin expedition had had several encounters with the "Esquimaux" but apparently did not seek their advice on shelter, food, and clothing. This was, after all, a journey fueled by Franklin's belief that he was the "protagonist in an epic story of high Victorian scientific triumph and colonial achievement."

I'm after something, taking the measure of this place

with my feet, with every sensory organ. When you're on vacation, different parts of your life collide with one another and you're actually holding still long enough to begin to notice some parallels. Ocean and Aquaventure and casino. River flow, casino flow, social-media flow, adrenaline flow. Screens: TV, computer, phone, aquarium window, slot-machine dashboard.

On the phone, Robert tells me he's been thinking about screens, too. He refers to them with the blanket term *rectangles,* because they are.

"Rectangles aren't found in nature," he says. "Maybe it all began with dividing up property," he speculates.

We are both quiet for a moment, mulling.

"Humans are hardwired to prostrate themselves in front of rectangles," he says. "I don't know where I heard that." Another long pause. "Maybe I just made that up."

QUARRY

During a spell of frigid February days, we revisited the quarries that had started us swimming back in July. We turned onto High Street, one of many narrow gravel roads winding into the pine and birch woods of Lanesville, where there are few houses but lots of granite, described by local historian Barbara Erkkila as ranging in size "from a squash to that of a house," and in shape from "great crags, spiny ledges and veritable small mountains of solid stone."

We were approaching a clearing in the woods, and there it was: Blood Ledge, which was once one of Cape Ann's largest, most productive quarries. Granite steps, like stadium seating for giants, led down to a lake of ice—about two hundred feet at its widest point—walled in by more granite. Erkkila, in her 1980 book, *Hammers on Stone,* has described Blood Ledge as "awesome"—back when the word still meant awe-inspiring, not merely cool. We stood at the quarry's edge, taking in the awesomeness.

Put any two people somewhere interesting and they will see it differently, in ways that are only partly explainable in words (in philosophy, they call this "the problem of other minds"). I'm drawn by the form, light, and color of things at particular moments. I was fixated on the pale olive green of the granite, pondering how color is never absolute, but a function of how light hits it.

Robert's attention, on the other hand, is laser-focused on even the faintest signs of human activity, and he's always reconstructing how things got to be the way they are. He pointed out a rusted iron loop sunk into the steamer trunk–size block a few feet away, and a tangle of rusted cable, nearly lost in orange pine needles. "That's what held the derrick in place," he said. Then he pointed out drill marks perforating one edge of the granite. They were about four inches deep and six inches apart.

"They made the holes with a star drill. Its tip was like the head of a Phillips screwdriver." He mimed the pounding and twisting action of manual drilling. "When they'd drilled a line of holes, they put in feathers and wedges, and then went down the line, tapping each wedge with a hammer."

"Wait, what's a 'feather'?" I asked.

"A shim. Two shims, one on either side of the wedge," he said. "Like a sandwich. The shims are the bread and the wedge is the meat: shim, wedge, shim. The shims distributed the pressure from the wedge being pounded down. Or it was like a sleeve, giving the wedge something smooth to slide against. Except the feathers didn't go all the way around."

"Too many metaphors," I said. "But I get it."

"Well, anyway. They went down the row over and over, all the while listening to the tones made by the hammer striking the wedge. It would get higher pitched as the wedges worked their way tighter and tighter into the rock. The idea was to keep the pressure even, so the stone would split evenly."

"How did they know when it was about to split?"

"I think it was when one of the wedges made a notably higher ring—that meant the stone had started the split. Also, because the split had begun in that one place, the other wedges loosened a little. The stone-cutter could hear and feel that looseness, so he tapped those down to match the one that had begun the split. It was kind of like tuning a guitar, a lot of listening and a lot of intuition. And slightly different kinds of granite behaved a little differently, so they had to take that into account, too."

This new process was a huge advance from the earlier method of splitting stone, which had involved fire and gunpowder—a method that could produce rough-hewn foundation blocks, wharf stones, mooring stones, and millstones, but not the precisely calibrated building blocks that resulted from the feather-and-wedge method.

By the 1830s, Cape Ann granite was being shipped to Boston and New York and all down the eastern seaboard. The pieces for each particular order were numbered; once on-site, they were assembled into some of the most significant stone buildings in America, including Boston's Longfellow Bridge; New York City's Holland Tunnel and the base of the Statue of Liberty; and the steps of the Washington Capitol. But these monuments weren't even the main part of Cape Ann's quarrying industry. An entire other sector of the industry emerged as America's population increased and more roads were needed. Paving stones became the larger share of the industry. Cape Ann pavers were shipped to New York City; New Orleans; San Francisco; Havana, Cuba; Seville, Spain; and Paris, France.

After a hundred years of boom times, quarrying on Cape Ann died in January 1930, just after the November 1929 stock market crash. The building industry was also changed by the advent of reinforced concrete, and paving stones were made obsolete by poured concrete and asphalt.

There's the macro version of an industry's rise and fall, and then there are the stories of hundreds of stone-cutters who, on the eve of the Depression, were suddenly out of work. Unemployment was devastating enough, but the disorientation went even deeper than that. It was the loss of the collective energy of a small army of men who had known just how to wield their bodies and their tools in the hard work of cutting and transporting stone. After the crash, they were no longer part of a team doing something important and profitable. The knowledge encoded in their minds and muscles was no longer so marketable, the material they'd wrestled with no longer a staple. Other industries would bounce back, but stone-cutting would become mostly artisanal.

On the way home, we drove past the entrance to the Babson Boulder Trail. During the Depression, a wealthy and eccentric financier, Roger Babson, had put unemployed quarrymen to work carving inspirational aphorisms on more than thirty large granite boulders in the Dogtown Woods. The sayings include: IF WORK STOPS VALUES DECAY; NEVER TRY NEVER WIN; and KEEP OUT OF DEBT.

We were approaching the eight-hundred-foot-long A. Piatt Andrew Bridge, which soars over the Annisquam River, connecting the island of Cape Ann to the adjoining mainland. Robert told me a story about our friend Zack Smith, a carpenter and a grandson of one of those last quarrymen.

Some years ago, Zack was tearing apart our neighbor's old deck. Tipped off by Zack, Robert had stopped by to haul away sections of the old decking so that he could repurpose them in our yard. Zack also needed to get rid of a very heavy granite step that didn't have a place in the plan for the new deck. He offered it to Robert.

Robert wasn't keen on hauling away anything weighing four hundred pounds, and said so. Zack pressed.

"After some more back-and-forth, it was clear that Zack didn't want this thing going in his truck," Robert said. "So I asked him why."

"It's not Lanesville stone," Zack had responded. It wasn't until then that Robert understood that *this* granite block was "from away." It could have been shipped up from South America. "I wouldn't have it on my property," Zack added, his vehemence mixed with disgust. "My boys wouldn't have it in their yards, either."

Robert said to me, "I was surprised he didn't say his unborn *grandsons* wouldn't have it. For him, it was just wrong to bring stone from somewhere else back to Lanesville. Like carrying coal to Newcastle."

Zack had, after all, lived in Lanesville all his life, surrounded not just by Cape Ann granite but by a Lanesville variant that was a pale fish-belly green, distinctively stippled with black. It was a hue and texture he knew as intimately as the faces of his wife and children.

It was the literal ground under his feet, and—perhaps it is not too much of a stretch to say this—part of his very ground of being.

In 1984–1985, more than fifty years after the demise of the quarrying industry, physicist Freeman Dyson delivered a series of lectures at Aberdeen University, in Scotland, addressing technology as "a force for good and evil in human affairs." He proposed that the technologies that have the greatest effect on human history are often the simplest. The harvesting of hay, for example, allowed nomadic populations to settle down and create stable communities. Once adopted, though, new technologies irrevocably alter the fabric of human life. "We cannot measure even in retrospect the human costs and benefits of a technological revolution. We do not possess a utilitarian calculus by which we weigh the happiness and unhappiness of the people who were involved in these case histories," Dyson wrote.

It wasn't until the last day of February, nearly two months after our swim on the day before New Year's, that we finally got back in the water. The dock at Conomo Point had been taken up back in October and would not be reinstalled until Memorial Day. We picked our way down the rocks toward choppy swells and gnarly cross-currents. Only our faces were exposed, and only between the eyebrows and just under the lower lip.

We slid into the deep middle of the channel, feeling the cold not just as chill but as insistent pressure. The buckling current swept us westward to the tip of Cross Island, where the blue house stood, its windows now battened down with plywood panels. We veered out of the current into the little cove below the house, our chests heaving, our gloved hands treading black water.

We lasted possibly fifteen minutes before turning and heading home.

LATE WINTER

The biggest storm of the winter roared across the Northeast on Monday, with howling winds and heavy snows that disrupted travel, education, and commerce. But it gave millions a day off from school and work, and transformed dreary landscapes to meadows of white in the portal to spring. . . . Meteorologists tracked the storm with the gravity of church wardens, but for millions of liberated children, and many adults, the realities were lyrics for a winter's day: awakening to a milk-white world, listening to snow falling in great hissing sweeps . . . walking down suburban streets draped in silhouettes, sledding and snowboarding in parks.

—*Boston Globe* (March 2, 2009)

Our "lyric" for that winter's day was a quick swim in Ebben Creek, which is not as foolhardy as it sounds. The creek is miles from the open ocean, has no surf, and its banks are just a few feet away should you need to get out suddenly. Snow—even dense, swirling snow—does not change the water in any appreciable way.

It was about three in the afternoon, nearing high tide. Unzipping the back of Robert's suit a few inches, I gave him his gallon of warm water. He did the same for me. We headed down toward the water, our wrists and ankles bulbous.

As I slid into the slushy creek, a little dagger of forty-degree water entered my suit, cooling off the warm water sloshing around inside so quickly that I knew we'd have, at most, ten or fifteen minutes to swim. I moved gingerly, not stretching my arms and legs any more than I absolutely had to, and entered a kind of snow globe: all white except for Robert's black hood and the black swoosh of his arm. I heard only my breath and my heartbeat.

But then: flashing lights, and the town of Essex rescue van backing up into Burnham Court, which dead-ends just a few feet uphill from the creek. The van's back doors flew open, spilling out men in yellow slickers and high black boots—the town's all-volunteer rescue squad.

Robert pulled himself up onto the snowy bank, stood, and gave a cheery wave. *Everything's fine. Nothing to see here.*

I waved, equally cheery, from the water. But it was clear they weren't going anywhere until we got out, so we turned back downriver, hauled ourselves onshore, and met the Essex police chief and several other volunteers at the bridge.

"If I were you, I wouldn't try to save me with those boots on," Robert said, breaking the silence.

Another long pause. "I've got kids, you know," said one of the men.

"We're pretty warm," I said.

"I'm freezing just looking at you," the chief of police snapped back.

A week later, we chose a swimming spot *not* visible from a state highway—the same spot off Concord Street, with its panoramic view of the entire Essex River Basin, where we'd first swum back in July. It was a Sunday morning, unseasonably warm for early March—in the high fifties. The tide was ten feet, seven inches, submerging everything except the marsh islands. We swam to the nearest of these, through bright sparkles of sun. Above us, clouds drifted toward the sea.

We hauled ourselves up onto the island, pulling off our fins, stumbling a bit on the shoreline, which was pocked with holes hidden under slippery seaweed. In the protected middle of the island, there was a stand of hickory trees, and the remains of a campfire. We found the island's highest spot, a pile of granite boulders scattered eons ago by the retreating Laurentide glacier. Waves lapped at the island's eastern shore.

"I wonder how long you could live out here without anyone noticing," I said.

"You could put a tent platform here," Robert responded. "And paint camouflage on the tent cover."

We were back in our recurring what-if game, speculating how we would survive if all we had was a little spot of land, whatever food we could gather or hunt, plus whatever tools we happened to have had with us when disaster struck.

We ticked off the obvious sources of food: clams, mussels, fish. Agriculture was out of the question: This island was mostly granite, with a small amount of soil supporting the weave of vegetation.

Online that night I found out that:

- Seaweed has long been used for the prevention and cure of scurvy, a dreadful disease caused by vitamin C deficiency. "'Depending upon the weed,'" I read aloud to Robert, "'that means you'd have to eat between 110 grams and 1.5 kilograms to get your RDA. That's doable, but not pleasant.'"

- Glasswort is also edible. "'As with most greens,'" I informed Robert, "'harvest when young and tender.'"

- Hickory nuts are even more edible; they are, in fact, the most calorie-dense and delicious wild plant food.

"How about fire?" I asked Robert a little later on. "Assuming we would have no matches or magnifying glass. Does it really work to rub two sticks together?"

"I've never actually done it," Robert said. "I just know it *can* be done. So that means it could be done by me."

SPRING EQUINOX

At a particular moment each year on March 19, 20, or 21, the Earth's axis is inclined neither away from nor toward the sun. Afterward, the northern and southern hemispheres switch places in facing the sun more directly. But in New England, spring's arrival can be agonizingly slow. Shorts and T-shirts one day, then a week of down-jacket cold. Snowdrops poking up out of the ground just in time to be obliterated by a blizzard.

The salt marsh is blanketed with dead cordgrass. Scattered bare spots—where storm tides swept away floes of ice—expose patches of soft gray mud. The color palette is still all bleached-out earth tones, with a few brushstrokes of maroon glasswort.

Although new *Spartina* will soon begin to sprout beneath this drabness, it will take many warm days for this new growth to begin the cycle of photosynthesis again.

During these early-spring days, there's a sense of life hanging in the balance.

On one of these gray afternoons, we swam Ebben Creek. The tide had just turned, but it was a "low" high tide, which meant there would be less time than usual to swim in high-enough water. We walked the marsh upriver, following the creek, picking an entry spot about a quarter of a mile up. That way, we'd have a good one-way swim back *with* the current.

Decked out in full winter neoprene, we crouched on the grassy bank, psyching ourselves up. We slid gingerly into the liquid equivalent of black ice, avoiding splashes. But then we were just happy passengers in a winding ride through the creek's bends and small landmarks. The willow tree and then the ash tree. The Christmas tree farm. The two Adirondack chairs. The little white toolshed up the hill.

The tide was dropping faster than we'd anticipated. Soon we were about a foot and a half below the grass line. I was floating on my back, not watching where I was headed, and bumped into a mud hump—soft and slippery and firm all at once—then ricocheted back into the darker, deeper ribbon of creek that is the last part to drain away at dead low tide. By and by, we felt the creek bottom soft as feathers against the tips of our fins.

THE RETURN OF GREEN

In the third week of April, we enjoyed several days in the high fifties and low sixties—air temperature, not water. Even toward the end of the month, Boston-area ocean temperatures hover in the low forties. We still needed our winter suits, but the warmer air at least meant we were no longer psyching ourselves up by pouring warm water into our suits before entering the water. In New England, spring arrives in these small subtleties.

We swam Ebben Creek with the current, under clouds that turned the water silvery blue. Around a bend: a sound like sheets snapping. A great blue heron with a six-foot wingspan lifted off over the tall grass, seeking more solitary hunting grounds upriver. Only slightly larger than the great white egrets, they are close biological relatives, diverging only down at the species level. Both species travel up the Atlantic Flyway—the ornithological equivalent of I-95—from the Florida Keys and South Florida. Both take the same off-ramp each spring to the Great Marsh, and spend the warmer months flying the same general local routes between the wide-open hunting grounds of the estuary and their protected rookeries inland. Their habits and general outlook on life are very similar, though the great blues tend more toward introversion.

Swimming with tidal currents can be frictionless, weightless bliss. But that all changes the instant you emerge from the water. The primary pull of gravity is downward again rather than sideways, and you also instantly lose the weight-reducing advantage of buoyancy.

With two arthritic knees, I was becoming more and more careful about climbing from the water onto rock. There were good reasons we'd started this swimming thing in midlife, why we were attracted to the weightlessness you often experience in the water, why we were so fascinated with the body-extending properties of fins and wetsuits.

In early May, new cordgrass sprouts are just on the verge of poking through the marsh lawn's winter wrack, but the overall effect is still overwhelmingly taupe and gray. My swim journal, on the other hand, was preoccupied with color.

5/1—Conomo Point. In at 6:20 and out at 7:40. Water spangled with sunset orange. We rode the current back. It's very localized, like getting on a road. You can see exactly where it is out in the middle of the channel by the slightly darker and, of course, swifter water. On the fast track, we zipped past boats on

their moorings, past yellow and red buoys. I'm
always drawn to the eye candy of colorful reflections. But there are other things going on, visu-
ally, with the surfaces of water. Besides reflection,
there's refraction and wave patterns. Sometimes
you see only reflection—what's above the surface of
the water; sometimes you see only refraction—the
filtered, bent version of what is down below. And
waves, or the lack of them, determine the topogra-
phy of what you see. If there are none, it's a mirror; if
there are ripples, you see things in long bands; if it's
choppy, everything breaks up into paisley.

At home, I googled "reflection and refraction,"
expecting science answers, but I got mostly instructions for graphic designers of video games and virtual reality on how to make photorealistic water
on-screen. "Adding Water" was one title. I read on:
"Water is a very complex shader inside of the Source
engine," it said. "With this complexity come rules
and restrictions on how it is placed and what sort
of water is used in different situations." Reading on,
I discovered that there is "expensive" and "cheap"
virtual water. Expensive water is, not surprisingly,
"the best looking." It will "reflect the world around
it, refract and fog the world beneath it (based on the
line integer through the water volume), and animate
a bump-mapped texture on the surface." Cheap
water, on the other hand, is for "situations where a

more simplistic water solution is called for." From then on, we sometimes referred to complexly reflective (real) water as "expensive."

5/9—Conomo Point: low tide, water temperature 59°. Under a milky lavender sky, we swam past the blue house into a little cove. Rocks studded with white barnacles, padded with seaweed. Green and gold and every shade in between. We gathered a bagful of mussels by feel. Later, washing the mussels, I found pearls just larger than grains of sand.

5/15—Conomo Point. A freakish temperature spike: it was 93°, and people were in bathing suits, sprawled in lawn chairs. To the north, Hog Island's deciduous trees had red-puffed tops, buds about to give way to leaves. The marsh grass was finally beginning to show in stiff threads of green piercing the old growth.

5/28—We celebrated our anniversary as we nearly always have, by walking the grounds of what used to be the Catholic retreat property in Ipswich where we were married. (Now it is New England Biolabs, which develops reagents for genomic research.) Miles River, a tributary of the Ipswich River, runs through the property.

We got our start in this watershed and have stuck with it ever since.

———❈———

There are few photos of that day, and only one shot of the entire wedding party. We stand in a semicircle under the densely purple canopy of a copper beech tree. Robert and I are exchanging rings, and promising lifelong fidelity to each other. We are both twenty-three, our faces smooth, our bodies taut.

My dress and the bridesmaids' dresses came from a department store. Our bouquets were rhododendron from Robert's parents' yard. We had bought four Pepperidge Farm vanilla sheet cakes, placed them on some foil-covered cardboard, and scattered flowers on the icing to obscure the seams.

Afterward, we all changed into shorts and played softball.

There's the iconic moment, and then there's the rest of your lives. We drove up to Boothbay Harbor to a waterfront cottage lent by friends of Robert's family, and set up housekeeping together. For dinner, we found half a package of Minute Rice in the backseat of our car, left over from the rice-throwing ceremony. Robert speared a flounder in the rocky cove.

A tendency that has stayed with us: to improvise with whatever is at hand.

This was more accurate than we knew: I was about a week pregnant at the time, hormonal activity altering my body even as we played backgammon and went snorkeling and climbed Mount Desert. After the honeymoon, I would feel the first twinges of morning sickness.

The heart begins as a single tube, a channel. There would be a moment, forever invisible and unrecorded, when that tiny organ tapped its first beat.

We had been aiming at careers as academics, and where we might have ended up after grad school is anyone's guess. But the clump of cells that became our first child had a kind of plumbline effect on both of us. By default we stayed in the area for the summer and just never left.

It rained for nearly all of June, except for the eighth, the thirteenth, the sixteenth, and the seventeenth. During that month, I fought off the anxiety that had stalked me ever since early childhood. I was sleeping fitfully. Even beautiful days would morph into burning intensity, accentuating the gap between beauty and my own ability to fully inhabit it.

It ran through my family like a river: My father had bipolar disorder, undiagnosed and untreated until just shortly before his death. My mother spent years self-medicating despair with alcohol. I had tried to run from the family tendency by moving from one end of the country to the other, and jumping into the Norman Rockwell painting that was Robert's family.

We swam Ebben Creek on another one of June's few beautiful days. Past both bends in the river, past the oak and the willow and the hammock and the peeling-paint

Adirondacks. Past two of the horses—the sable and the Appaloosa—past the place where once we saw a snapping turtle slip into the water with barely a splash.

The channels got curvier and shallower. I flipped over onto my back, and Robert steered me lightly by my foot. I held my breath for buoyancy and floated through clouds.

Weeks later, it would be like a fever breaking. I slept, and gradually began to forget what it had been like to be in that other stifling place.

In early July, the sun finally came out and stayed out. In just our bathing suits, we swam channels that had been heating up all day in the sun. We swam past birds in a frenzy of eating and mating: The cardinal jumping from fence post to fence post, his red not a solid red, but many reds, a moving flower. Then the Baltimore oriole's glorious fluorescent orange.

When we got home, Robert dug up the first new potatoes of the season: little orbs ranging in size from marbles to robin's eggs to golf balls. I washed them in the sink, trying not to rub off too much of the paper-thin red skin.

WALKING TO THE BOTTOM OF THE TIDE

On the Fourth of July, we drove a few miles west of Ebben Creek to a three-hundred-acre tract of low marshland surrounded by Castle Neck River and Hog Island Channel. It was a beautiful day—wind riffling through the marsh lawn, ultramarine sky with fair-weather clouds. The tide was about an hour away from dead low.

An egret landed ahead of us, disappearing into a slot in the green. We wore knee-high muck boots, clumsy approximations of the egret's bright yellow feet, because today we were hiking, not swimming. Our goal was a rectangle suspended in heat shimmer about a mile away, a one-room hunting camp owned by friends of friends, who used it mainly for duck hunting in the fall. If you didn't know about the complex vascular system of tidal marshlands, you'd think you could walk straight to the camp in about fifteen minutes. But we'd be navigating a labyrinth of channels and ditches.

We set off between the shoreline and the deep channel to our right. Our boots crunched on springy, thick mats of hay interwoven with dried seaweed, bleached crab skeletons, pieces of lobster-pot rope, and random boat bits. Here and there were floes of marsh mud that had been lifted up and redeposited by storm tides.

We took a slight right onto a path leading away from shore and wove our way around salt pannes— small, shallow pools that sheltered mummichogs and sticklebacks, the shorebirds' equivalent of McNuggets. When these tiny fish felt our footsteps, they shot under canopies of pink- and ocher-colored algae. In a few spots, the algae had spilled out onto the ground and bonded with marsh grass and dirt. I loosened a piece and picked it up. It was like half-dried homemade paper, a weaving of land and sea.

The path ended at a hut woven of saplings and reeds, a structure several steps up from typical duck blinds, which are often just fifty-five-gallon barrels sunk into the ground, with sticks and thatch in front of them to hide the hunter. This one had two chambers: the blind itself, with a chair and a roof; and an enclosure that held a small rowboat and a dozen or so decoys. In the fall, they would bob and drift in the pool a few feet away from this outpost of human habitation.

We followed a barely discernible path across a series of ditches that were spaced like yard lines on a football field. You can't do a running long jump in muck boots, so I got into a rhythm of throwing my arms forward, ready to grab the grass to secure my landing.

After that, it was just a confoundingly serpentine maze of creeks. The only way forward was mindfully. We couldn't head straight for the camp without being blocked by channels, but we had to veer to the left of it, using a boathouse on the inland side of Crane Beach as a kind of lodestar. We hiked another half mile toward the boathouse, like sailors tacking toward a compass point.

The back side of the camp began to show faint details; this was the point where we knew we could shift course and head straight for it—clear hiking for the last quarter mile. We picked up a path that led to the front of the shed-roofed camp, its shingles weathered silver. It was up about six feet on pilings, and had a shallow front porch.

Robert pulled a key from his pocket and sprang the padlock to the front door. As we stepped inside, the room flooded with light, revealing canned goods crowded onto a single shelf, a propane cooktop, a small sink, and bunks with army blankets thrown over bare mattresses. I picked up a zippered book, which was actually a container for playing cards and a pad of notepaper divided up into two columns: "Us" and "Them." Robert was paging through a logbook with dated entries from the owners and their family and friends: who had been there, how many ducks they had shot. He seemed to be looking for something and not finding it.

Back outside, we sat on the deck, legs dangling, eating our heat-soft cheese sandwiches. We passed a water bottle between us, leaving a few inches for the walk back. We had underestimated our thirst.

From where we'd begun, Hog Island had been a drumlin-shaped icon of forest and fields and hedgerows, an improbably high spot in the middle of the ocean of marsh. It also contained, like a nesting doll, a smaller, lighter green hump near its middle. But up close, the icon had deconstructed. The hump was actually Dean Island, a completely separate landform. Much of the height of the island was due to the spruce trees that had been planted back in the 1920s by the financier Cornelius Crane, who had loved the spruce islands up in Maine and wanted to reproduce that here. But he'd planted them too close together, and they were beginning to die off. There were gaps like missing teeth in the row of them along the island's crest line.

An airplane droned overhead, a pinpoint in the cerulean sky. All was heat and quiet. Even at high tide, this was a secluded spot, an inlet within an inlet within an inlet, generally only found by the handful of people who own the place or are allowed to use it. But now, the tide reduced to a trickle, not even the lightest of kayaks could be paddled right to this hunting camp's front door. Out in the channel's middle, a narrow band of water was still flowing. I knew the ground was relatively firm there, and I wanted to walk into a vastness that was something more than just acreage.

"I think I'll go down there for a little while," I said. "Just walk around a bit."

Robert raised an eyebrow. "I think I'll stay right here."

Barefoot, I climbed down into a wet, oozy version of the Grand Canyon, half-sliding down its erosion-formed crevasses and buttresses. My foot broke off a big chunk of creek wall. The creek bottom, on the other hand, was all unstructured, unbound stuff, the remains of pretty much anything that had ever lived and died here: grass, fish, crabs, shrimp, dinoflagellates, algae. It was the color of bittersweet chocolate, flecked with fragments of shell and straw. My right foot plunged past the top few inches of warm mud into cooler layers, a slippery enveloping. My left leg sank in a little farther, to mid-shin. Arms outstretched as if I were walking a tightrope, I eased the right foot out of its hole, stepping ahead into mud a few inches deeper still.

My two feet were mired at different heights and awkward angles. I considered. On the one hand, the sandy middle of the channel was only twenty feet away; on the other, it was hard to judge where the pockets of very porous mud might be lurking. My human center of gravity was all wrong here. So were my feet, evolved as they were for upright travel on firm surfaces.

Up until this moment, I had not particularly noticed the periwinkles, the marble-size, striped-shell snails that inhabit the creek beds by the thousands. Now I saw that they were moving, slither-roaming at a rate just under my normal threshold of motion detection.

Bending very carefully, I picked up a snail and watched its little trapdoor open and swivel (what a feat of engineering these little creatures are!). First the undulating black foot unfurled, and then the head poked out, stretching and waving. Though I knew I was only a flash of information to the snail—a generalized largish possible threat, seen through something like a pinhole camera—it was one of the few times in my life I've felt I shared a gaze with a nonmammal. There was nothing mystical going on, just a sober-minded acknowledgment of fellow creatureliness across a chasm of scale.

I emerged from the creek wearing muddy knee-socks. I rinsed off as much mud as I could, in a shallow pool near the camp. Robert was right where I had left him—on the front deck, legs dangling.

"I'm so glad I didn't have to go in and rescue you," he said.

Sitting down beside him, I told him about the snail. "What's the most memorable time you've ever made eye contact with an animal?" I asked.

He did not hesitate. "It was a snowy owl. Did I ever tell you about that?"

"It kind of rings a bell, but tell me anyway."

"I was out cross-country skiing after dark and was headed back to the workshop," he said, meaning our business workshop in the middle of the West Gloucester woods. "I'd left the lights on inside, so the windows were glowing. I heard this huge crack, and a few seconds later, a heavy thunk. It was a branch breaking off one of the white pines, followed by the load of snow that had built up on the branch."

Then he'd noticed the pile of snow moving, and something emerging: a snowy owl about two feet tall, with a catlike white face and a fluffy brown-stippled body. It flew straight for the closest window but hit its head on the glass and tumbled back onto the ground.

"I had this sinking feeling it had broken its neck, but it roused itself and flew to the window again. This time, it landed on the ledge, but the ledge was so skinny, it couldn't really perch there. So it spread its wings"—he stretched out his arms to indicate a wingspan of five feet or so—"and kind of pressed itself into the window."

There was a fire going in the woodstove inside, and no storm windows to block the heat radiating off the glass, so the owl just stayed there. Robert had crept inside, tiptoeing closer and closer to the window until he and the owl were nearly face-to-face. Its pupils had shrunk to pinpoints; its eyes were blazing gold circles.

"I don't know if it saw me," he said. "I just stared at it for a long time, and it hardly moved. I don't think it even blinked."

Down below, my footprints were already beginning to fill and soften with water. The tide had turned when neither of us was looking.

Later that evening, Robert was at the iMac.

"Oh," he said softly.

I peered over his shoulder. Using Google Earth's "history" filter, he'd conjured up where we had just walked as it had looked in 2006. The satellite shots had all been taken in the winter; the Essex River Basin was a study in earth tones, etched with white.

"There's the duck camp," I said, pointing out a faint rectangle.

"But it's not where it's supposed to be."

In the winter of 2006, he explained, ice had built up under the camp and fused with the thick floes that were covering most of the marsh. During a storm tide with strong winds, the camp had loosened from its pilings and been carried to a spot about two hundred yards away. Weeks later, about twenty-five men, including Robert, had formed a crew, and, with sheets of plywood, levers, rollers, and a block and tackle, moved the camp back over a period of two days.

"Basically, it was the same process as moving stones to build the Egyptian pyramids," Robert told me. "It went *very* slowly." The first day they'd gotten the camp about halfway back, and the next day they reached the original site, where they heaved it onto a rebuilt and stronger foundation, with two-by-tens nailed to the base to stop ice from getting under the foundation again. "So the satellite photo could only have been taken at the end of the first day, with the camp at the halfway point."

"Amazing." Google Earth creates the illusion of an eternal present, but it is, of course, a patchwork of satellite snapshots of radically particular moments in radically particular places. Sometimes it catches a strobelike moment of transition.

I looked closer and saw two rectangles: One was the camp itself, and the other, fainter one was the imprint of where it had been before the storm. Between the two rectangles were the curved tracks of a large object having been pushed across the marsh. It was a bit of script, a fragment of an algorithm, a human mark that had come and gone.

FULL CIRCLE

A few days after our Independence Day excursion, one of us happened to notice that it had been exactly one year since we had started our swimming practice. Like many milestones, it was anticlimactic. We kept swimming the rest of the summer and just past the fall equinox.

But in early October of that year, Robert had rotator cuff surgery, followed by weeks of recovery. Getting used to colder and colder water during the fall had been the on-ramp to winter swimming, and we missed it that year. The following year, he had the other shoulder repaired, followed by an even longer recovery. This time, we weren't even looking for the on-ramp.

As it turned out, we did not use our winter-weight suits again. We still swim in the warm months—around here, that's roughly from late May through early October—and still sometimes use the lightweight suits and bootless fins for that.

For what we paid for our collection of suits and fins, we probably could have flown to Europe and back. But it was a bargain. The habit itself was the point, and that stayed with us no matter where we were. (It's not for nothing that the word *habit* is closely related to the word *habitation*.) The journey continued in different ways in the years that followed. It became a template that opened up ever-larger questions about our estuary and its watershed neighbors both near and far.

The same suits that transformed our bodies into sleek water vehicles became a vehicle for what Edmund Burke termed "the moral imagination," that capacity through which "we build up a sense of the world with the aid of symbols, metaphors, images and associations of various sorts," an "imaginative whole or framework" that "influences profoundly how we think and act."

Sometimes that process takes you back to earlier parts of your story: to remember; to reconstruct; to correct, as needed. And sometimes it drives you to update your itinerary for the next leg of your journey through time and space.

PART 2

A watershed is a gatherer—a living place that draws the sun and the rain together. Its surface of soils, rocks and plant life acts as a "commons" for this intermingling of sun, water and nutrients. . . . For humans, the watershed is a hydraulic commons—an aquatic contract that has no escape clause.

—Peter Warshall, "Streaming Wisdom:
Watershed Consciousness in the
Twenty-first Century"

GROUND TRUTH

We were all of twenty-five, with a baby, the year we sank a concrete foundation into a wooded parcel of land in West Gloucester. The land included a small body of water somewhere between swamp and pond, and a fifty-foot change in elevation up a granite wall. To the west lay dense woods that had once been Tink Newman's woodlot.

We'd been reading books about house building, along with the *Whole Earth Catalog* and *Mother Earth News,* and had decided the house would have no central heating. Its southern exposure would be mostly glass; a masonry floor would absorb the sun's heat during the day and release it at night. A small woodstove would fill in on cloudy days.

As soon as the ink was dry on the deed, Robert raced to get the house enclosed—exterior walls up, roof done—before winter set in. The electric company could not hook us up until January, so Robert rented a generator for a few days to cut all the two-by-sixes into joists and rafters, and the plywood into sheathing. It was like a pile of Tinkertoy parts. Two friends were helping the first month or so. The three men worked mostly without electricity, and mostly in bitter cold. Roof shingles froze and snapped.

A woman with an infant is no help at a construction site, so baby James (he would later go by "Jim") and I were at home in our winter rental ten miles away most of the time, with no car. Days as a young mother can go by very slowly, especially when the baby doesn't nap much and dusk falls at 4:30. A yellow backpack saved my sanity. It had a sturdy padded belt that rode low on the hips and cinched snugly, a feature that made possible long walks over rough terrain with a big, active baby. Outside on the hilly streets of Annisquam, the world opened back up for both of us. I sometimes felt like a two-headed being, with two sets of eyes and ears, as we cut through the backyards of unoccupied summerhouses and hiked down to an ice-crusted beach.

We moved into the house when it was barely habitable, and managed to get to church the next morning, a little rumpled. The church had what I can only describe as open-mike time, though its official name was Sharing and Prayer. Robert took the mike briefly to announce that we'd "run our ship aground" in West Gloucester. People who'd been there for years, whose parents or grandparents had worked the quarries, saw us a little differently after that; we were no longer in that category of college students and seminarians "from away" who rotated through every few years and then spun off somewhere else, seldom to be heard from again.

Flipping through the *Whole Earth Catalog* one night, I came across a quiz assessing how aware you were of the bioregion where you lived. The rationale for the quiz was that in order to live well and responsibly, you needed to be familiar with the ground that—both literally and figuratively—supported you.

- When you turn on your faucet, where does the water come from? When you flush the toilet, where does the water go?

- What soil series are you standing on?

- How long is the growing season?

- What are the major geological events that shape your bioregion (faults, uplifts, downwarps, volcanics, sea floods, etc.)?

- How many days until the moon is full?

- From where you are sitting, point north.

I knew only two of these six—and those were just a few of the questions. But over the months that followed, we began to know our plot of land through sheer exposure, much of it involving digging. No matter where you dug, eventually you'd hit granite. Above the ledge, the soil was mostly clay. Only one spot in the entire parcel, in fact, had passed the "perc" (percolation) test that certified the soil was porous enough for a septic leach field. We'd dug a shallow well and hit water just ten feet belowground, but many of our neighbors had drilled wells, tapping into a much deeper water table. We dug footings for a deck, and found a buried stash of bricks, the remains of a brickworks. The straighter ones eventually found their way into a primitive backyard patio. In planting a lawn and garden, we wrestled with greenbrier—*Smilax rotundifolia*—and began to wonder if there might be one massive taproot lurking underground somewhere in West Gloucester.

All around us, like benevolent giants, eastern white pine—*Pinus strobus*—grew fast, tall, and straight. We'd thinned the pines to make room for the house, then thinned them some more to expand our yard and open it up to sunlight. A neighbor with a tractor hauled the logs into a pile, inadvertently rototilling long tracks into the woodland floor. The next spring, seeds that had been dormant—perhaps for decades—sprouted in these tracks: ferns, maple seedlings, buttercups.

Our daughter, Mary, was born in March 1980. Robert hammered together a bedroom for her the day before, a baby-size alcove at the top of the stairs, with a built-in crib and a tiny skylight. Because he'd built the house from the ground up, he regarded it as infinitely malleable, putting up walls and taking them down as our needs changed. (Our third child, David, would be born in 1986.) Children slow you down. ("This is a 'walk,' Jonathan. Not a 'stand,'" I recall one of our friends saying acerbically to his poky two-year-old.) We had leapfrogged over the phase many of our married friends had enjoyed—living and working in a big city for a few years before having children and moving to the suburbs—trading that for intense knowledge of a specific place. Instead of the Hudson or the Charles or San Francisco Bay, we had Walker and Lufkin Creeks, and the Essex River Basin. Instead of Central Park, we had the West Gloucester woods.

Since Robert and I still shared a car in those early years, my trips into town were few. My world shrank to a circle whose radius was the approximate distance I could cajole two small children to walk in an hour or less. As we walked, we named the landforms and landmarks: the Stone Table, the Big Rock, the Crooked Tree, the Little White House.

One summer day, the children and I climbed over the stone wall at the edge of our yard and just kept walking along the Great Ledge, one of the many Silurian period outcroppings of Cape Ann granite. It rose like a stegosaurus above a lobe of wetlands, then tapered off at its eastern side, where it stopped at the freshwater edges of Walker Creek.

By then, Mary had taken her brother's place in the

backpack; three-year-old James was down on his own. We hiked the edge where rock met earth, but it was a complicated, messy edge, strewn with boulders and fallen trees, and slippery with leaf meal. As we made our way, the pine grove gave way to beech and swamp maple, which gave way to cattail and then freshwater reeds— indicators of the transition from woodlands to brackish wetlands and then, finally, to the salt-marsh lawn ahead of us. The grass pressed down in cowlick patterns where deer had stopped to rest.

The morning fog had burned off and we'd come a long way for James, who, after all, had to take two steps for every one of mine. We'd go back by way of Concord Street, a much quicker path home. But it was time for a break. I slid the backpack off and parked it on the grass. Easing Mary out, I set her down and took her hand while she got her land legs back. The three of us walked over to where the grass overhung the channel, watching Walker Creek meander through mud toward a bright spot about a half mile away—one of many small portals into the Great Marsh, where the grass stretched for miles to the horizon.

It isn't often that you're down in an ecosystem's substrate, its basement. In the years before we began swimming the tidal creeks regularly, we'd mostly just passed through the marsh at high tide in boats, on our way out to the beach. In very hot weather, we'd occasionally jump into the deepest pools for a quick dip—but again, always at high tide. The water was always the point, not the muddy structures that contained and channeled it.

Students in drawing classes are often told to draw the spaces between the solid parts of some dauntingly complex object—an old-fashioned handheld eggbeater, for example. The technique works surprisingly well. Because you have fewer preconceptions about what the in-between spaces "should" look like than about the object itself, you are bolder about drawing them. The end result is a fairly accurate-looking eggbeater. This new way of seeing figure and ground was transformative for me as a young artist.

Something similar transpired during the swimming year. The Great Marsh's 200,000-some cubic acres of living and decomposed organic matter, its matrix, was becoming the very thing I wanted to know more about. I began to grasp how foundational the *Spartina* grasses were to this matrix. Because they are so salt-tolerant, they compose the lion's share of that organic matter. Their roots have a specialized membrane that can pull water into the roots of the plant but filter out most of the salt. And, like bamboo and raspberry plants, they are rhizomatous, sending out underground stems that produce roots below and send out new shoots above. This is how the marsh cordgrasses can colonize a shoreline for as far as conditions are right, often for miles.

Structurally, the salt-marsh substrate is a rhizosphere—a soil region both created and perpetuated by plant roots.

By definition, you can't ever see a rhizosphere whole. But you can peer into it by breaking off a hunk of creek wall and pulling it apart. Inside, its dark, peaty stuff is bound together with the pale yellow gnarls and filaments of cordgrass roots, a structure that answers the question of how marsh walls can be so relatively lightweight and yet hold their shape so well, how spongy and soft can also be strong. You can extrapolate from these traits to see why a healthy marsh is a shock absorber for much of a wave's energy, a flexible but sturdy front bumper for the edge of a continent. You see how it traps and binds together plant remains, silts, and clays, forming spaces and interstices—habitats—for life-forms ranging up and down the size spectrum.

You hold in your hand the very definition of a matrix: an environment, material, or structure within which something develops. And salt-marsh peat is an environment for many organisms, which—unlike the birds, fish, and mammals that visit this intertidal zone but have their primary residences elsewhere—are lifers. Some, like the ribbed mussels in their lonely creek-wall hermitages, you can easily spot. Some you can barely see, like the nematodes—the tiny worms ranging in size from microscopic to about the width of a grain of sugar. They feed on cordgrass roots and live in the upper layers of marsh sediment, along with blue-green algae—single-celled organisms that produce oxygen through photosynthesis. You can't see the individual algae (under a microscope, they resemble strings of turquoise beads), but you can easily see them collectively as shimmery, slimy masses.

Immediately below this "oxygen horizon" are the purple bacteria, which have a highly idiosyncratic habitat preference: They cannot live in oxygen, but since they are photosynthetic, they must be close to the surface, near the light. Farther down, conditions are increasingly dense and decreasingly oxygenated. To see what lives here, you'd need a core sample and a microscope.

So much of what lives in the marsh peat is very, very small. Once past the first skim of earth, you are into the realm of prokaryotes—single-celled organisms that have no nucleus or other specialized organelles (organized or specialized structures within a living cell). Digging further involved, for me, a crash course in microbiology, where things got confusing very quickly. The last biology class I'd taken was freshman year in high school, back in 1968–1969, when, as far as I knew, there were only two main divisions of life: animal and vegetable.

It wasn't until the 1970s that scientists began sequencing DNA, allowing them to classify organisms not only by their physical characteristics and ecological roles but also by their cell genetics—a breakthrough that resulted in life now being divided up into three domains: eukaryotes (organisms encompassing both plants and animals), bacteria (one-celled organisms lacking a nucleus), and Archaea (distinguished from bacteria by their genetic makeup and by their ability to survive in extreme environments).

DNA sequencing required new imaging technologies—new lenses, if you will—that opened up windows into the very small inhabitants in this peat ecosystem. Other key technologies, developed in roughly the final one-third of the twentieth century, would reveal in unprecedented detail the intricate processes—biological, geological, and chemical—going on in these tiny worlds. These new technologies include nuclear magnetic resonance imaging—one of the most powerful tools in modern science. As its name implies, it provides information on environmental processes at the molecular level.

It's interesting to note that John and Mildred Teal's landmark study, *Life and Death of the Salt Marsh,* first published in 1969, mentions storm protection, pollution filtering, and support of species diversity as benefits of this ecosystem, but it does not mention marsh peat as an unequaled reservoir of "blue carbon"—the term for carbon captured by the world's ocean and coastal ecosystems.

Scientists have known since the eighteenth century that the Earth is a carbon-based planet, and that the Earth's carbon exists in six basic "reservoirs": rocks, ocean, atmosphere, plants, soil, and fossil fuels. But the more powerful tools and lenses of the late twentieth and early twenty-first centuries have allowed them to go deeper. We now know that the plant biomass that thrives in coastal marshes (both as live plants and, even more, as decomposed material underground) "sequesters" carbon—that is, it stores carbon in a reserve form, counterbalancing the greenhouse gases—mostly airborne CO_2—that are responsible for climate change. Since the Industrial Age—with a significant spike following World War II—human activities have tipped the balance between carbon reserves in the ground and carbon dioxide turned loose into the atmosphere.

Preserving effective "carbon sinks," like estuarine marshes, is a hedge against the effects of all the carbon we've extracted from the ground and sent into the atmosphere. Although coastal habitats cover only a small percentage of the total ocean area, they provide about half of the carbon sequestered in marine sediments.

In other words, the ground under your feet in a marshland—these "blue carbon" reserves—contains buried treasure, a crucial part of the entire biogeochemical economy of the planet.

Put healthy toddlers down in an outdoor environment and they'll do one of two things: run or dig. I'd taken my eyes off mine for all of thirty seconds, and now both were squatting at the edge of a shallow salt panne, plunging their tiny fingers into the oh so soft and slimy muck, trailing tendrils of green algae. Mary's nearly new Stride Rites and James's little sneakers were an inch down into it, and my knee-jerk response was to pluck them both up to higher ground. It was almost lunchtime, then nap time—the blessed hour or so each afternoon when I'd be off duty for a while. All mothers look forward to nap time, but introvert moms especially so.

I hesitated just a moment too long. Mary stood and took another step into the center of the pool, the mud swallowing up the high tops of her shoes. So I sat her down, tugged off the shoes and socks, and rolled up the legs of her overalls. I did the same for James, and we all went down into the nearly empty channel, where the mud was relatively firm but still squishy enough to feel good underfoot. I was barefoot, too.

The children were scooping holes in the muck, then watching the water level seep into them again. I picked up a twig and set it in a trickle of creek.

"Boat," said Mary.

I spotted some chips of brick, the same stuff we'd found in our backyard. They'd been made from veins of clay that can be found here and there in the marsh mud. I made a little enclosure with them. It might last for a tide or two.

Little ones who are taking a "stand" or a "sit" instead of a proper walk are onto something. They are parsing out for themselves what time, space, and matter are all about. It is the most primary of primary research. They're not thinking of the Earth's biogeochemistry, but they're taking in its properties even so, learning why salt-marsh mud—squishy, spongy, indelible on clothing, inconvenient for human transport or other enterprise—is a *good thing,* worthy of their full attention.

A LONGER VIEW

We didn't know it during those years we were raising our family, but just one watershed north of us, scientists had been carrying out long-term research on salt-marsh ecosystems for years—decades, actually.

Plum Island Sound is an ecosystem researcher's Shangri-la. It's a megawatershed, with three substantial rivers flowing into it: the Ipswich, Parker, and Rowley Rivers. In 1998, the site became one of the National Science Foundation's Long-Term Ecological Research projects. It's part of a network of twenty-eight such research organizations nationwide, and one of only four specifically doing sustained site-based studies of human effects on salt marshes.

Anne Giblin, lead scientist of the Plum Island site, and also the director of the Marine Biological Laboratory's Ecosystems Center, is a marine biologist whose current research examines nitrogen and carbon cycling in estuaries. Sandy-haired, with a warm, crinkly-eyed smile, and generally dressed for field work, Giblin got her first taste of collaborative long-term research in 1975, when she was among a group of graduate students exploring the

Great Sippewisset Marsh, in Falmouth, Massachusetts. Their professor had been performing marsh-fertilization experiments, a study that had begun five years earlier, and would continue into the future. Nitrogen fertilizer makes lawns grow lush and green, but it also drains seaward, and ends up fertilizing *Spartina*—accelerating its above-ground production but sometimes reducing its critically important belowground biomass accumulation.

From then on, Giblin was hooked on long-term collaborative science, and her early career took her to research sites as far away as Alaska's Toolik Field Station. It takes a particular kind of scientist to stick with a project for decades, and to share both the limelight and the eventual authorship of the results. Long-term ecological research, in other words, is no career for divas. Environmental trends develop slowly in response to climate change, and it takes ecosystem-scale data gathering and experimentation to uncover trends. The payoff is information that can't be gotten any other way.

Along with ongoing studies of the effects of nitrogen runoff, two forty-foot information towers track the "breathing" of the ecosystem. Various sensors are mounted on the towers, which monitor the physical and chemical properties of the relevant atmospheric processes. Among other data collecting, they measure carbon cycling—the process by which marsh biomass absorbs carbon dioxide, "sequestering" it so it cannot enter the atmosphere and morph into environmentally harmful greenhouse gases.

The Plum Island site's mission is threefold: Along with research, it is also devoted to education and community outreach.

That was how I found myself at the Marshview Farm Field Station, just off the Newbury Turnpike in Newbury, Massachusetts, for an open house sponsored by the organization: "Celebrating the Great Marsh and Its Watersheds." It was a beautiful early-October day; the marsh, stretching for miles all around us, was still mostly green, the grass rippling in the breeze. It was an outdoor, family-friendly science fair, with posters and tables full of displays, the colorful variety indicating the breadth of organizations conducting research here.

I wandered around, checking out the displays. "Nowhere to Go: Can Plum Island Marshes Survive Sea-Level Rise?" one display was titled. To survive, marshes must build elevation by gaining biomass at least as fast as the sea level increases. I scanned the photos and captions, and found a photo of a sediment plug—an experimental sample of marsh peat. It looked a little like a two-layer wedge of chocolate cake, with a white icing-like strip separating the layers. The whitish layer, I read, was residue left over from a marker horizon set into the marsh sample from about four years earlier. So the top layer was the past four years' accumulation of peat.

Another display presented facts and current research

on the alewife, a fish that migrates yearly from the ocean to the rivers where they were spawned. They're an important part of the ocean/estuary/river food web, but they are threatened by overfishing, degradation of river habitats, and dams and other obstructions that block their migratory passage. Still another display traced the effects of a warming and acidifying ocean on soft-shell clams' shell development. A team of animated, articulate high school students presented results of their field research on the invasive perennial pepperweed.

I paused at a model of what happens to waterborne pollutants when they sink into the ground. It was like a big version of an ant farm, with the "soil" held between two sheets of glass. This presentation had happened earlier, before I'd arrived, but when Anne Giblin noticed me and a few others bent over the model, trying to figure out how it worked, she joined us for a repeat performance. She poured a little colored water into a tube. It sank into models of wells and other openings in the soil. "When liquids go down into the ground," she said, "you would think they'd just sink and stay close to the area where they entered. But here's what actually happens." The colored water was spreading laterally, finding its way downhill toward a body of water. The visual aid showed the drift of water, including waterborne pollutants, into aquifers, and eventually toward estuaries and oceans. Those of us gathered around were mesmerized, and Giblin paused, letting the visual aid work its magic. One member of this audience, who lived nearby, mentioned factories that used to operate in Newburyport back in its more industrial days, and how the runoff from these industries must have ended up in Plum Island Sound.

Giblin seized a teaching moment. "It's so important to think about all of these things—not just what's happening here at the edges but everything going on upstream, as well." She gestured expansively, indicating the entire watershed: from its inland woods, suburbs, and urban areas to this verdant, surprisingly resilient continental edge.

NASSAU, AGAIN

Near the end of a flight from Boston to Nassau, at about the same latitude as the Florida Keys, the first signs of the Bahamian archipelago slide into view. The unearthly aqua is the shallow bank (generally less than thirty feet deep) surrounding each island, and forming the edge between these continental shelves and the sharp drop-offs into deep ocean. The next color ring is the bone white of exposed beach, followed by the green of mangrove swamps—the subtropical and tropical counterpart to the cordgrass marshes in the temperate zones. The middle areas of the islands, the slightly higher elevations, are the variegated greens of *Lignum vitae*, Caribbean pine, and various kinds of palms.

First you cross over Bimini, the northeasternmost of the Bahamian islands. Then the Berry Islands, and then New Providence. The island's shoreline, especially its one deepwater port, is encrusted with hulking, gleaming cruise ships and hotels, which from the air do not look all that different from the power plant that supplies electricity to the island, and the "seawater reverse osmosis plant," which produces millions of gallons of freshwater each day. They are all part of the same economic loop.

After three hours of being airborne, I emerge into warmth that can be felt even through the Jetway, happy I left my down jacket behind. It will be there for me when I return, ten days from now.

The first year the five of us were here, we ranged in age from fifty-five to sixty-six. Now the span is from sixty-six to seventy-seven. More often now, the conversation turns to joint pain and when to get knee-replacement or cataract surgery. We worry a little more than we used to about the husbands we have left behind to fend for themselves.

Yet overall, our routine here is so similar from year to year that we date them most easily by the big events we saw on TV at night during a particular trip. The first year, the only year we came in January, we watched Barack Obama sworn in. In March 2013, we saw Jorge Mario Bergoglio introduced to the world as Pope Francis. In 2017, a mid-March storm halted most flights back to Boston; I managed to fly as far as Charlotte, North Carolina, and bunkered in an Extended Stay motel for two involuntary vacation days.

This year, Hurricane Dorian—whose 185 mph winds missed Nassau but flattened big swaths of the Abacos—is only half a year past. The memory of it is still raw.

There are storms back home we're tracking, as well. In a few days, we'll be watching the results of the Democratic Super Tuesday primaries. COVID-19 is increasingly in the news. Our president downplays the severity of the pandemic.

Several of us snorkel every chance we get, even when the water is choppy, as it is today. We're tossed around with the sea fans and the schools of blue-and-white sergeant majors. The tangs are a molten blue, and the queen angelfish has the colors of a peacock's eyes. And then there's the aqua-and-pink iridescence of the stoplight parrotfish, the harlequin purple and yellow of a damselfish. The names alone feel good on the tongue and in the ears: fairy basslets, yellowtail snappers, wrasses, bar jacks, hamlets, banded butterfly fish. A spiny lobster's antennae and flagella poke out of a rocky hermitage. A brown-and-white Nassau grouper slides behind a velvet curtain of brain coral.

Here it's not hard to remember that all life on Earth began in water, with soft creatures that were not even cellular yet, floating atomistically in primordial seas. Later life became unicellular, followed by "soft animals of great complexity [that] preceded animals with hard parts, just as soft people making artifacts of great complexity preceded knights in armor with their hard parts." The jellyfish floating by is a descendant of those soft animals. If they wash ashore, though, they are utterly helpless.

Today I'm especially noticing the reef itself, with its exuberant variations on the theme of coral: mustard hill coral, finger coral, brain coral, staghorn coral. Fans and whips and horns. Yellow and blue and purple and red. It's as if Frank Gehry, Dr. Seuss, and Simon Rodia got together and collaborated on this.

But the builders and maintainers here are actually polyps—that is, the tiny jellyfish living inside the individual limestone pods of this collective. Each species has a different aggregation algorithm, if you will, which determines whether the coral will be branching or blobbing or doming or spiking. Their colors are determined by the particular type of one-celled algae living inside the polyps' bodies. When the animals die, they leave behind their pods, and new polyps build on the old structure, a process that, over many years, can build up a vast reef.

And reefs are the bedrock of these coral islands. Like other habitat-building species, they weave together land and sea, providing both storm buffer and habitat. Suspended in the water as a human visitor, you can see the waves slowed by crevasses and tunnels, by rough, reticulated surfaces.

Though coral reefs take decades, even centuries, to mature, they can be destroyed by just a few seasons of higher than average water temperatures. The destruction is called "bleaching," and it refers to the shock reaction in the overheated corals: They expel the colorful algae living within them. Reefs can survive a few bleaching events but will eventually die off.

Out of the water, I go for a walk along the beach, idly picking up white stuff: bleached coral, Styrofoam fragments, small chunks of concrete, and the perfectly formed edge of a plastic cup.

AREAS OF CRITICAL ENVIRONMENTAL CONCERN

There is no place on Earth where human presence does not cast a shadow. Not even at Ebben Creek. Route 133 bisects it and compromises somewhat the free flow of the incoming and outgoing tides. *Phragmites australis,* an invasive reed, grows in the disturbed strips of land where the road was excavated and where houses have been built. The reed outcompetes native cordgrasses and provides few ecosystem services in return.

Parallel grid-ditching scores the marsh throughout the Essex River Basin, along with nearly all of the coastal marshlands from Maine to Virginia. Most of these 562,000 miles of trenches were dug during the New Deal era by Civilian Conservation Corps workers, with the goal of controlling mosquitoes by draining salt pools, where the larvae tend to develop. The ditching has not, in fact, been effective in reducing the mosquito population.

During the year we swam this creek frequently, we began to notice small erosions in the salt-marsh lawn where we'd taken shortcuts. We swam over stubs of foot-ings that used to hold up docks. We noticed salt pools too rectangular to be natural—maybe they'd been used as impoundments for fish.

Then there are the diminishments, the gradual attritions of species. The piping plover and saltmarsh sparrow, for example, are both threatened here. I know from my neighbor Deborah Cramer that horseshoe crabs (*Limulus polyphemus*) were once abundant in Walker Creek. "Each spring at the highest high tides, they used to come out of the mud to mate and lay their eggs," she writes. "The creek nursed the young crabs, and they stayed in its embrace all summer. With each molt, they left an unblemished shell on the shore. This year I found just one shell."

Old-timers have told us that oysters used to be so plentiful that the local creek beds were thick with them. We can still find them, but it's a long trek across marsh lawn to a few rocky channels we know about. We don't take many; they are a special treat.

Some losses are so long past that you have to be told about them. Take the luxuriant beds of eelgrass that once blanketed these wetlands below the *Spartina alterniflora* zone—underwater, in other words. Eelgrass, which dis-appeared from the Great Marsh back in the 1950s, curbs the erosion of bottom sediments and provides protective habitat for shellfish and juvenile fish. Any loss of habitat will reduce the diversity of species found in these waters.

And then there are the losses that blindside you. For example, when you go to Conomo Point to gather mussels after a few years of falling out of the habit, and you discover they are greatly diminished. It makes no sense; they have always clustered in blue abundance on rocks and pilings. But the green crabs—*Carcinus maenas,* a European invasive—have devoured them.

And yet these are relatively small problems compared to what has happened to wetlands elsewhere along the New England coast, not to mention the fate that has befallen coastal wetlands nationwide. Since Colonial times, approximately half of the nation's salt marshes have been dredged, filled, and built upon. My home state of California has lost between 75 and 85 percent of its original coastal wetlands. Los Angeles, my birthplace, has lost over 95 percent. (This is why, though I was a Californian from 1954 to 1976, I never knew what a salt marsh was until I moved east.)

The Great Marsh has many advocates, however. In the wake of coastal storm damage caused by Hurricanes Sandy (2011), Harvey, and Maria (both 2017), six Massachusetts cities and towns—Salisbury, Newburyport, Newbury, Rowley, Ipswich, and Essex—drafted the Great Marsh Coastal Adaptation Plan. Spearheaded by the National Wildlife Foundation in partnership with the Ipswich River Watershed Association, the plan "assesses regional and town-specific vulnerabilities to current and future coastal threats and identifies near and long-term ecosystem-oriented strategies that reduce risk and increase target resilience."

The Great Marsh is still considered a jewel; we who live here are privileged to have this unusually intact marsh to enjoy, to study, to restore where needed, and to plan on behalf of. When you're out in the middle of the Essex River Basin, standing on a spit and taking in a full-circle view of largely undisturbed beaches, marshes, and islands, it can be hard to grasp that it all could have turned out quite differently here.

Like the Velveteen Rabbit, perhaps, places become real when they are loved. I do not mean to say that the marshlands north and south of us are less loved by the people who live in them, just that "our" Great Marsh has been loved by a range of entities—national, state, local, and nongovernmental—that have had the vision, the power, and the funding to protect it. The Massachusetts portion—from Gloucester to Salisbury—was designated an Area of Critical Environmental Concern in 1979. The ACEC declaration, in turn, had grown out of a long-standing ethos of environmental protection in Massachusetts. It was the first state, in fact, that adopted regulations protecting wetlands—seven years before President Nixon signed into law the National Environmental Policy Act.

Until fairly recently, I did not know this: that in 1970, MEPP Inc., an organization of twenty-nine Massachusetts Municipal Electric Departments, presented the town of Ipswich with a proposal for a nuclear power plant at the end of Town Farm Road, which runs about two miles northeast from Route 1A into uplands that look out onto an expansive view of Plum Island Sound, just north of us. Because nuclear generators need vast amounts of water for cooling, they are nearly always sited by rivers and coastlines. The proposed site was one estuary north of the Essex River Basin, near the beach colony of Jeffreys Neck, in Ipswich.

I stumbled on this information on the blog Historic Ipswich, written by Gordon Harris, town historian. "The Board of Selectmen," Harris writes, "'realizing the need for information as to the safety of such an operation, financial arrangements with the Town, rise in water temperature at the outlet of the cooling system, and the ecological performances of the plant,' appointed a nine member Nuclear Power Plant Advisory Committee to conduct a study, submit a report to the Board and gather information in order to bring the issue to a vote." (MEPP had, in fact, been scoping out the town of Ipswich as a potential power plant location since 1964).

For the next year, the town engaged in a mostly civil debate. One of the materials advanced by the pro-nuclear side was a diagram showing the huge pipes that would pass beneath Plum Island and discharge into the Atlantic. It was "intended to assure Ipswich residents that Plum Island Sound would be unaffected by thermal discharge," Harris writes.

In the end, the proposal was soundly defeated at an Ipswich town meeting in 1971. Harris's blog post includes a contemporary photo of Seabrook Station as seen from across Brown's River. "[T]his would have been the view from Jeffreys Neck Road," he writes.

Seabrook, New Hampshire, got that view instead. And the New Hampshire portion of the Great Marsh became an asterisk.

If you didn't already know what it was, Seabrook Station today could easily be taken for a university campus with an observatory, or the back side of a cluster of big-box stores. At any rate, it is now indelibly part of the landscape, visible from both Seabrook Beach, just over the line in New Hampshire, and Hampton Beach. These are both barrier beaches, and, like Crane and Wingaersheek, are separated by a channel of several hundred feet, where the Atlantic Ocean flows in and out of Hampton Harbor and its several thousand acres of marshes.

Robert and I have just hauled our kayaks down a gravelly bit of shoreline across the bridge from Hampton Beach State Park. We push off into Hampton Harbor, paddling past moored fishing boats, headed toward a verdant swath of marsh where John Fogg and his family harvested marsh hay to feed their livestock up until the middle of the twentieth century. Hay was a valuable commodity back then, and so was this marsh acreage.

I have read Fogg's little book, *Recollections of a Salt Marsh Farmer,* which he began writing at the age of eighty-seven. In it, he recounts the history and practices of salt haying that had been passed on to him from his father and grandfather. I have pored over his map of the Hampton Falls and Seabrook marshes, which shows the paths and landmarks of that long-gone way of life. I have compared it with Google Earth aerials of the place. All of the curves and bow bends of the creek are pretty much as they were a century ago.

From kayak level, it looks like any tidal estuary. Brown's River zigzags toward the mainland, as tidal creeks habitually do. All around us are marsh islands, hardly distinguishable from Corn, Cross, and Dilly Islands in the Essex River Basin. "I think that might be Hunt's Island," I call out to Robert.

The twin nineteen-foot-diameter rock tunnels—one bringing seawater from the ocean to cool the reactor, and the other returning the used water about a mile offshore—are invisible, because they are sixty-some feet underground.

We paddle farther up Brown's River, passing abandoned pilings that were once boat docks.

"Maybe that's where 'Nate's Stake' was," I muse, half to myself, squinting into the sun at an oxbow bend in the creek. The stake had been as big as a telephone pole, and it had served as a gathering place for the haying teams, which usually started out at a landing at the end of Rocks Road—the Rocks, for short.

We will not reach the Rocks today, or any day. The plant is built on the uplands that terminate there. We round another creek bend and paddle up close enough to read the exact wording in which we will be told we cannot go farther:

SECURITY ZONE

IN ACCORDANCE WITH 33 CODE OF FEDERAL REGULATIONS PART 165.33, ENTRY OR MOVEMENT WITHIN THIS ZONE IS PROHIBITED UNLESS AUTHORIZED BY THE CAPTAIN OF THE PORT, PORTLAND, ME. <u>NO PERSON</u> MAY ENTER THE WATERS WITHIN THE BOUNDARIES OF THE SECURITY ZONE UNLESS PREVIOUSLY AUTHORIZED BY THE CAPTAIN OF THE PORT OR HIS AUTHORIZED REPRESENTATIVE.

Robert paddles in a wide loop about forty feet into the forbidden zone, because he can. I shoot him a wifely eye roll.

In the late 1960s, Public Service New Hampshire had begun its purchase of upland in Seabrook, along with adjoining marshland. John Fogg sold his marshland to

PSNH in the early 1970s, after the town of Ipswich had NIMBY'd the nuke. "With the clearing of the plant life and excavating of the land there," Eric Small writes in his introduction to Fogg's book, "he was struck by the reality that this area, of which he had such fond memories, was being destroyed before his eyes. He wanted to preserve for posterity the life he had known there during his early years."

In February 1972, PSNH applied to the New Hampshire Site Evaluation Committee for approval of the Seabrook site for a nuclear generating station.

In June 1978, Robert, James, and I had played an extraordinarily minor part in a protest at the future site of the Seabrook Station, twenty-six miles and two watershed addresses north of us. We were worried, of course, about what a reactor meltdown could do to this place we were beginning to call home. We went to the Alternative Energy Fair, a precursor to the actual protest the following day, and wandered the dusty construction site along with throngs of other mostly young adults, checking out the exhibits and picking up flyers (think Renaissance Faire, minus the costumes). Pete Seeger sang an adaptation of the old folk song "Acres of Clams" ("I expect to live here till I'm ninety/It's the nukes that must go and not me").

What followed was a protracted struggle between pro- and anti-Seabrook factions that dragged on until one of the original two reactors finally went online in

1990. It was a time line that included, on the one hand, two nuclear disasters elsewhere in the world—Three Mile Island in 1979 and Chernobyl in 1986. But because apocalypse in our backyard did not happen, we sort of forgot about it. It was overshadowed by the overwhelming immediacy of day-to-day life with small children.

Seabrook Station is about a half mile away from us now, and I am struck by how much it looks like the modernist architecture that had been pervasive in Southern California during the postwar years. That aesthetic is in my blood, right up there with eucalyptus trees and the Pacific Ocean and the wide-open spaces of the Mojave Desert. Along with the reactor itself and its surrounding complex of concrete squares and rectangles, there's a silver structure that looks like a Buckminster Fuller geodesic dome. I am finding the whole thing weirdly beautiful, and the surprise of it all makes it easier to consider this estuary, also, as my own.

Because every place, really, should be an area of critical environmental concern.

CHANNELS

One of the ironies of swimming and kayaking is that we often drive to get to our favorite spots, for two reasons: to conserve precious after-work time, and because it's often getting dark by the time we're out of the water.

One of us slips the key into the ignition, foot poised above the accelerator, the first step in a convoluted process of gas and air igniting inside the pressurized chambers of the car's cylinders, creating the force that moves the pistons that turn the driveshaft that turns the wheels that propel the machine—a four-thousand-pound hulk of iron, aluminum, plastic, glass, rubber, copper, and steel—forward. This key-turning, accelerator-pumping moment, this translation of heat energy into kinetic energy, is a portal into another channel, a river formed not by the flow of water, but by humans going about their business.

Now we are traveling Eastern Avenue, which threads together the islands and peninsulas of the western edge of the Essex River Basin. Until the early 1600s, this path was trod only by Native Americans. Then came the British settlers, whose wheeled carriages and market economy thickened and hardened the path into a road. The bridge over Ebben Creek was first built in 1700, and the gray house directly across Ebben Creek from Farnham's—long before there was a Farnham's—belonged to Ebenezer Burnham, a boatbuilder. By 1800, farms, mills, icehouses, and the shipbuilding industry sent more and more traffic over this bridge. Essex-built schooners got goods to market faster and faster; at its peak, this tiny town was a major manufacturer of fishing vessels.

Eastern Avenue became part of Route 133 in 1960, giving commuters easy access to Route 128, where, in 1961, Collaborative Research would be established as the first biotechnology company in Massachusetts. Our segment of 128 (from Danvers to Gloucester) was the final part to be completed, in 1959.

Continuing south, we'd be time-traveling from Essex—whose main industries are now tourism and shellfish—to Boston's world-class array of universities, research hospitals, think tanks, financial firms, and biotech companies. In less than an hour, we could find ourselves on the 270-foot-high, quarter-mile-long Zakim Bridge, navigating a channel of blurred asphalt, streaks of other cars, flashes of sun on the windows of high-rises, and billboards advertising coffee Coolattas and divorce lawyers and ice-cold Coke.

If there's no traffic, it can feel like flying, like what psychologist Mihaly Csikszentmihályi has termed "flow": that state we attain "when self-consciousness is lost, one surrenders completely to the moment and time means nothing."

However, the faster we go, the more complex and costly the vehicles we must buy or borrow to attain these velocities. The more effortlessly we travel, the less we can see the ground underneath us, which bears the unpaid costs of our fuel and channels and vehicles.

(And do not discount what might seem the most trivial of vehicles: the plastic cups and containers that make it possible to drink and eat while we drive. They are cheap, and they disappear from our lives in a flash, but they pile up as an unfathomable debt in landfills and oceans.)

Several times a year, we take a convoluted shortcut off the Southeast Expressway on our way to Logan International Airport. We pass Bill Wainwright's whimsical, light-reflecting sculpture, *WindWheels,* at the intersection of Neptune Road and Frankfort Street on our way to the North Service Area Roadway. We leave the car in long-term parking, hop on the shuttle, enter the terminal, and nearly always get to take another shortcut, the TSA PreCheck line, because we are old now.

This week, we have flown from Boston to New Orleans—sixteen hundred–some miles—to spend the week with Jim, Susan, and our three grandchildren. They live north of the city, across the twenty-four-mile-long bridge over Lake Pontchartrain. For an eight-mile stretch in the middle, you lose sight of land and, if you didn't know better, could believe you were at sea.

All week we've been immersed in the children's needs and, even more important, their loves and obsessions: Peter's leaf collection, Henry's and Annabelle's Legos, which occupy much of the square footage of the floors of both their bedrooms. They are all in school for the day, so we're free to chase an obsession of our own: to get as close to the mouth of the Mississippi River as possible. We've flown over it when our flight takes a southern approach into NOLA, and want to see it for ourselves, this liminal edge where floodwaters and sediment from thirty-one states fan out into the Mississippi River Delta and dissolve into the Gulf of Mexico.

We are many miles and one time zone west from the tank farms of Boston, at the extreme other end of a petroleum-delivery channel that begins in these various locations all along the Gulf of Mexico, Louisiana prominent among them. Louisiana is one of the top oil-production states in the nation, with seventeen refineries that can process 3.3 million barrels of crude oil per day.

We're headed due south on Louisiana Highway 23, miles now beyond the New Orleans city limits. We will not see another Subway or Burger King or Dollar General until we return. The river is to our left, but we can't actually see it; it's hiding behind a grassy twenty-foot levee. We see the occasional tops—the masts and derricks—of large freighters. To the west, also unseen behind a parallel levee, are the wetlands and barrier islands of Barataria Bay and, beyond that, the Gulf of Mexico.

What we do see is rich deltaic farmland: citrus groves, a vineyard, cattle sprawled under live oaks. Towns with idiosyncratically named streets and businesses (Carol Sue Avenue, Washateria, Fix-a-Fone). The farther south we get, the narrower the land and the closer together the levees. Side roads stretch enticingly toward hidden marinas and sportfishing cabins for rent.

We share swigs of water and a bag of pork cracklings (we have never had them before). We're in our default mode, mostly just looking, using words as necessary.

By the time we reach Venice (population 202, zip code 70091), the road has lost its shoulders and there are no more levees, just land edging toward water in all directions. We take a right onto Tidewater Road, which is aptly named: Egrets and herons and brown pelicans stand, laconically, in water that has swamped the road. Just beyond the last of the pavement, anticipating the few who venture this far, a sign reads:

WELCOME

YOU HAVE REACHED
THE SOUTHERNMOST POINT IN LOUISIANA
GATEWAY TO THE GULF

We do not park the car, exactly, just turn off the engine and get out. Our glasses, cooled by the air-conditioned SUV, fog up immediately. We breathe in the smell of salt water, wet pavement, and creosote.

This is not really the southernmost point of Louisiana, of course. It is merely the farthest you can get in a land vehicle. From here on down, water will increasingly dominate land, and zip code 70091 will feather out into seemingly infinite islands and bays, these tiny roads replaced by shipping lanes and seaplane routes.

About ten miles south of where we stand is Head of Passes, which is the river's mile zero. Here the river spreads out and divides into three tributaries. Collectively, it's known as the "Bird's Foot Delta," the youngest lobe of the ever-evolving Mississippi.

Aside from a few industrial buildings to the left side of the road, we really could be in Essex. We're many miles from the mangrove swamps, and into grassland. The species that dominate here are *Spartina alterniflora* (its common name here is oyster grass) and black rush, *Juncus roemerianus*.

It's all the same basic stuff—water and mud and grassy low islands and shorebirds—just so much more of it. Some 40 percent of the contiguous U.S. coastal wetlands are right here, in fact: three million acres, or about 4,500 square miles of it all around us. It dwarfs our own marsh's forty square miles.

We see little evidence, on this beautiful summer

day, that Venice was devastated by Hurricane Katrina in August 2005. Or that in the summer of 2010, oil from the Deepwater Horizon explosion began washing ashore in the community.

I hear a distant *yung-yung* of a motor, which could be from a powerboat or even a chain saw, but I immediately think of the Jet Skis that break into the tranquility of too many summertime idylls in the Essex River Basin and elsewhere.

Until quite recently, these personal watercraft (PWC) had two-stroke engines, which are so inefficient at burning fuel that they dump as much as 30 percent of it, unburned, into the body of water. Their only function is to be a one-person boat that can travel thrillingly fast, yet small enough to maneuver into shallow areas and small inlets that regular powerboats cannot reach. They are perhaps the most flagrantly frivolous use of the internal combustion engine.

And yet . . .

That four-hour flight from Boston to Louisiana, at a rate just under the speed of sound, and with an energy cost of approximately one gallon of fuel per second. These seventy-five miles we've come down Highway 23 in a two-ton, 400 hp SUV. We're Jet Ski riders, too. It's been a long and expensive journey to get here, to stand awhile in the heat and stillness of what seems like the very edge of the world, and to contemplate the contradictions of our lives as members of the brilliant and rapacious species *Homo sapiens.*

Back home, the Great Marsh's acreage is holding fairly steady. But every few years, Louisiana loses the equivalent of one Great Marsh.

Heading back into Boston, we cruise over Cape Cod, over leafy South Shore suburbs. Then the plane loops out into the Atlantic briefly, then turns and heads toward the nearly sea-level runways of Logan International.

It takes some imagination to picture what Boston Harbor was like in preindustrial times. Downtown Boston was a 470-acre peninsula protruding into the harbor, and the entire Back Bay area of the city used to be salt marsh. The airport was built over what used to be four hundred acres of salt marsh in East Boston, which lies between Winthrop to the northeast and downtown Boston to the southwest.

What is now East Boston was once five inner-harbor islands—Noddle's, Hog's, Governor's, Bird, and Apple—surrounded by water. Now those islands are a conglomerate, joined by fill. Chelsea Creek flows between East Boston and the city of Chelsea toward Somerville, where it merges first with the Mystic River and then the Charles, flowing through the inner harbor out into the open waters and scattered islands of the outer harbor.

In satellite view at least, Chelsea Creek can look like

a cousin of the Essex River. But its edges and surrounding land are crowded with infrastructure that contains and distributes the Commonwealth's industrial lifeblood: gasoline for cars, salt for the roads, and home-heating oil. And, of course, the jet fuel for the approximately six hundred flights per day departing from Logan Airport.

The Creek is considered to be, according to text from the website NOAH—Neighborhood of Affordable Housing, a 501(c)(3) nonprofit dedicated to improving the lives of Massachusetts residents—the most contaminated tributary flowing into Boston Harbor, and the second most polluted body of water in the Commonwealth. The group notes, further, that "Chelsea Creek is the source of more environmental and public-health burdens than benefits" for the largely working-class and immigrant residents of Chelsea and East Boston. According to Professors Daniel Faber and Eric Krieg's report "Unequal Exposure to Ecological Hazards," these two areas rank third and fifth, respectively, as the most environmentally overburdened communities in Massachusetts. It was time for us to take a baby step toward environmental justice by paying a visit to our watershed neighbor.

It's about one o'clock on this mid-July day, and I have pulled to the side of the road on Fenno Street in Chelsea, Massachusetts, 2.5 miles from Logan. The trees overhanging both sides of the narrow street make it seem like a grotto. Though this little neighborhood hugs Route 1, it is largely hidden from it, separated by chain-link fencing and the kind of wild growth—somewhere between shrub and tree—that grows lush and viny during the warm months in these parts.

To my right is a boom gate, and beyond that, a path that disappears into a dense shaded strip of land running along the embankment of the southbound side of Route 1. Looking down the street half a block or so, I can see just the legs of a man lying on a creeper seat, working on the underside of a car. If I were a different sort of person, I would go say hello, would ask if it's okay to take just a short walk past the boom gate. But I am not that sort of person. It is less a fear of strange men than an inability to explain to anyone, really, why I am here and what I am looking for.

Robert and I will be kayaking Chelsea Creek tomorrow, and I'm on something of a reconnaissance mission, scouting around for somewhere along this 2.6-mile-long waterway to park a car and to carry two kayaks down to the water.

It's surprisingly challenging to find such a spot, but any resident of Chelsea or East Boston could have told me as much. Though these cities are nearly surrounded by water, there's little public access, making it difficult for residents to enjoy their waterfront, let alone curious outsiders.

And now I've gotten sidetracked, drawn into a maze

of obscure streets, driven by some inchoate need to see for myself where Chelsea Creek begins. Actually, this far up the waterway, it's called Mill Creek; it will join Chelsea Creek about a mile east. I know in a general sort of way that creeks begin as ponds or other elevated drainage areas. And I have figured out, more specifically, that such a pond once existed in the acre or two of land where, just about a mile from me now, Routes 1 and 16 meet in a heavily traveled figure-eight interchange. The map on my phone shows a wavering line of water running across one grassy loop, then passing under a culvert to another one, where it follows the same pattern: culvert, feeble stretch of creek, another culvert, and then it passes under asphalt again, reemerging as a straight line of water running along Route 1 for about a quarter mile before it disappears into a grid of streets.

And, as the car idles, I'm somewhere near that vanishing point. But I can't get there, at least not without trespassing and possibly triggering a 911 call from a concerned passing motorist.

My next stop is the Parkway Plaza, where on my phone I've spotted the creek meandering between this shopping mall and the Revere Beach Parkway. I park behind Home Depot, near a loading dock. I can't see the creek from here, though, just more chain-link fence and, behind it, a tall thicket of interwoven trees and underbrush.

But up ahead, past Home Depot, there's an opening in the fence, and friendly-looking signage. The sign,

printed in both Spanish and English, reads: WELCOME TO
MILL CREEK RIVERWALK, CHELSEA'S NATURAL TREASURE,
A REMNANT OF THE LUSH SALTMARSHES THAT ONCE
COVERED CHELSEA RIVER. POLLUTION AND NEGLECT
ALMOST DESTROYED IT, BUT CONCERNED CHELSEA CITI-
ZENS TOOK ACTION.

I pull my phone from my back pocket. Searching
"Mill Creek Riverwalk Chelsea MA" brings up a page
from the City of Chelsea website:

Park Type: Walking, Jogging, Nature

Size: 0.554 acre

Management: Chelsea Commons
Management

About Mill Creek:
Mill Creek and connecting Chelsea Creek
are important habitats for both marine
life and shorebirds. They are a spawning
ground and nursery for smelt, American
eel, Atlantic butterfish, Atlantic cod,
Atlantic mackerel, Atlantic sea herring,
pollock, red hake, and at least four types of
flounder. Many birds who feed on the fish
hatchlings—such as egrets, swans, herons,
and cormorants, are therefore attracted to
these estuaries to feed and breed.

For the first several hundred feet, though, the Riverwalk is a narrow asphalt path running between two chain-link fences, and the growth is so thick that I can see neither the creek nor the back side of Home Depot. There's a sound like rushing water, but that's the traffic up on the parkway.

Then the fence on the creek side disappears; through the trees—sumac, shagbark hickory, aspen—I can glimpse the creek, so lush and green, I could be back at home. The loopy bends are just the same. It smells the same. I almost don't notice the upside-down shopping cart stranded on a bit of muddy creek island.

Farther down, there are benches, and a woman on her phone, who turns from me. I keep walking, but still farther down, nearly hidden in shade, is what I recognize as a tarp, the outside wall of a shelter. I turn back, partly out of fear, but mostly out of respect for the precarious peace of a stranger.

Back out on the sidewalk of Revere Beach Parkway, I find just the right spot: Cronin Skating Rink, a public facility overseen by the Department of Conservation and Recreation. It's public enough that Robert and I should be able to park here without being questioned. The large lot slopes down to a clear swath of creek. Not the kind of shallow, sandy bank I'd prefer for easy entry, but close enough.

Then a gaggle of Canada geese—large brown bodies, black necks, and heads with white cheek patches that make the heads look a little like saddle shoes—turn in unison, necks extended, beaks wide open, scary little serrated tongues waggling, protecting clutches of eggs that are, no doubt, tucked away somewhere between the underbrush and the water.

The next day, it takes me only a few minutes' paddling from the skating rink to notice that there are jellyfish in the creek, hundreds of them scattered around in small floating groups. Their bodies are translucent as plastic sandwich bags, except for a more opaque body part consisting of four circles in a loose cloverleaf arrangement. We paddle through dense stands of reeds. I float over a submerged mud and algae–covered tire, and veer around another upended shopping cart, water flowing through its orange plastic sluice. A school of tiny fish follows me for a few seconds, then does a collective left turn and darts beneath the kayak.

Up ahead, Robert's kayak trails plumy red reflections. Mine is blue. Both are old, left over from back in the nineties, when, as a side venture, we helped start a kayak-touring business in Essex.

"The mill's coming up ahead," I call out to Robert. Paddling an urban creek in ninety-degree heat was perhaps not what he had been planning for this day, but I have enticed him with one of the oldest tidal mills in New England, Slade's Mill, originally built in 1735. It was one of many such mills on tidal estuaries, where you could bring your corn and have it ground in exchange for a "miller's dole," a percentage of the final product.

We approach the three-story brown-shingled building jutting out into the creek. It has been converted into apartments but maintains its original footprint. We paddle through the passage between the building's stone foundation and the built-up rectangle of land on the other side of the creek.

"This is where the waterwheel was," Robert says as we enter the rock-walled flume. And then, pointing with his paddle toward the opposite bank, he adds, "That was the foundation for the axle on the other end of the mill."

Out on the other side of the flume, we paddle into a wider channel, the tide still rising. We pass between abandoned granite piers that once held up a steam-era rail line connecting Chelsea with Lynn, ten miles north. Just a few minutes upriver, we time-travel as we duck into the slatted shade of the current commuter rail line.

Up ahead is the mouth of Mill Creek, where the waterway makes an abrupt right turn, merging with Chelsea Creek and widening even further.

Since Colonial times, Chelsea Creek has been flanked by working industries, many of which used and still use the channel to transport raw materials and finished goods. The river is officially classified as a Designated Port Area: a stretch of waterfront set aside primarily for industrial and commercial use.

To the east, on the Chelsea side, we skim past a cluster of abandoned brick warehouses, windows long since gone. A small brick smokestack stands near a newish-looking wind turbine. Mill Creek's muddy banks have, by now, given way to a solidly vertical edge of corrugated steel, rusty with long exposure to salt water, and scored with faint white water lines. Yellow signs forbid shellfish harvesting.

We are now in industrial big-sky country, land of oil-tank farms, where bargefuls of refined petroleum arrive daily at marine-vessel docks, their cargo transferred into the above-ground storage tanks that loom on the landscape like a fatter, shorter version of Midwestern grain silos. On the Revere and East Boston side of the river, Global Partners, LP, rules. It is one of the largest gasoline distributors and transporters in New England and New York. On the western side, the Chelsea side, it's all Gulf Oil.

Up ahead, Robert has paused mid-channel, the kayak equivalent of idling. I pull up alongside, laying my paddle across both of our bows so we can float together for a while.

He's intent on something, peering into the heat shimmer of water and buildings farther upriver. "The drawbridge is starting to go up," he says, meaning the Chelsea Street Bridge. I've seen it before, mostly on 1A on the way to Logan, but never like this, at sea level. From here, gazing straight on, the bridge looks like twin lighthouses, except for the small fact that I can see sky through their truss construction.

The whole street section begins to rise, not splitting as a drawbridge would, but remaining whole and parallel with the ground. The bridge turns into a low-slung H, then a normal, equilateral H, and finally, when the street is 175 feet up, a giant white croquet wicket. It's a vertical-lift bridge, raising this entire four-lane section of Chelsea Street by means of cables and concrete counterweights.

Robert speculates on the cables, what kind of metal they are, whether they are bundled strands or woven, more like a belt. He has to think about these things, just in case the universe needs someone, at this exact moment, to be alert to the properties of this machinery.

A riffle of bow wake approaches the bridge. Several minutes later, a cheery red-and-yellow tugboat comes clear—two tugboats, in fact, both of them hovering close to an enormous oil tanker, like border collies herding Holsteins.

We paddle aside, toward shore, and wait as the entire tug-barge unit plows toward us, hull and cranes and railings and ladders and pump rooms, black and yellow and red.

"I wonder what the draft is," Robert says, shouting over the engine's roar.

"The what?"

"The depth of the barge. The part below the waterline."

We watch the barge head upriver, toward the Gulf and Global tank farms.

"Looks like it's making a U-turn," Robert says. "That'll take a while."

We continue on toward the bridge, which is back in its normal position now, traffic swishing back and forth again. Just before we slip underneath it, I notice a person way up in the tower, like a Lego figure wearing a gleaming yellow hard hat. I wave, but the figure remains still, implacable.

On the other side of the bridge, I paddle toward the waterway's first real stretch of green since Mill Creek. It is the Condor Street Urban Wild, a 4.5-acre park built over a contaminated industrial site formerly owned by the Hess Oil Corporation. It is East Boston's only public park on the Chelsea Creek waterfront. I have visited it on foot, have climbed its zigguratlike hills and stood at the railings of its fishing pier. I'm drawn to urban oases like this one, to the vision and tenacity they represent.

On the opposite side of the creek is another oasis, this one sharing space with the Eastern Salt Company, which owns and operates the park in partnership with a Chelsea neighborhood organization. A playground made of oil tanks, surrounded by lush plantings, stands next to Eastern Salt's several forty-foot salt mountains. Robert and I paddle past, peering up at an amphitheater made of an old loading rack. We hear the rumblings of feet and a basketball.

"Do you want to keep going?" Robert asks.

On the one hand, I'd like to paddle just a bit farther, out to the confluence of Chelsea Creek and the Mystic River. On the other, the tide will be turning soon, and I'd rather go back with the current instead of against it.

"Here is good," I respond, reverse-stroking to turn my kayak.

I head for the abandoned brick building hugging the opposite shore. I'd seen it only from a distance on our way up, and been struck by its classical proportions, especially its tall Palladian windows. Until a few years ago, it had housed one of the last working steam engines in Boston, which had pumped sewage to the Deer Island treatment plant offshore. NO TRESPASSING signs have since been bolted to the brick.

Upriver, the barge has docked at Global, tended by a team of men whose job it is to manage the supply pathways between these oil tankers and the storage tanks onshore. They wave to us as we paddle by.

Between the tanks, we can just make out the start-and-stop traffic up on Route 60, most of it headed toward the airport.

A 747 drones far above us, headed west. And we meet our own gaze out the airplane window.

AIRBORNE

Early in the morning of the day I am to fly to California for the wedding of a childhood friend, I swim Ebben Creek, hoping to neutralize the effects of six hours in an airplane seat. At this hour, the creek seems like a reverse image of itself, everything lit from the opposite direction.

Later, I slip into my usual window seat. For the first few minutes, the view below is of Boston Harbor, made up of five watersheds—the Charles, Mystic, Neponset, Weymouth, and Weir River Basins.

Less than an hour later, after crossing the spine of the Appalachians in Pennsylvania, we pass over the invisible line that separates land draining east to the Atlantic Ocean from that draining west and southwest to the Mississippi River and the Gulf of Mexico.

I spot Pittsburgh, and convince myself I can make out the spot downtown where the Ohio, Allegheny, and Monongahela Rivers converge. A few miles east of that spot is the University of Pittsburgh, where my father entered college in the fall of 1939, working summers in the steel mills to pay his way through.

I'm seeing just the upper reaches of the Mississippi River watershed—at 1,245,000 square miles, it touches thirty-two states and covers 40 percent of the landmass of the continental United States. It has five major tributaries and many smaller ones.

When my father worked in Pittsburgh's mills, it was barely more than a decade after the Great Mississippi Flood of 1927, which covered 27,000 square miles in thirty feet of water. It had actually begun in the summer of 1926 with catastrophic rainfall ten times heavier than normal. Under more normal circumstances, the forested land could have held a lot of that water. But for the first quarter of the twentieth century, untold acres of trees had been commercially clear-cut. Without trees and their deep roots, the soil could not do its "ancient work" of absorbing floodwater after seasons of intense snow and rain.

The velvety greens of the Mississippi River Basin gradually give way to the Great Plains' tallgrass prairie, and then to shortgrass plains farther west. The landscape flattens and dries out. Before the early twentieth century, 180 million acres of these native grasses covered the entire plains. Like the saltmarsh cordgrasses, prairie grasses sink their roots deep into the soil, and about 85 percent of the vegetative biomass stays underground.

During the same era that the Mississippi River Basin's forests were being clear-cut, farmers in the plains were "deep-plowing" the native grasses and virgin soil.

Demand for American wheat was high during World War I, which accelerated the agricultural takeover of the region. On the eve of a prolonged drought that would plague much of the 1930s, slightly more than half of that original ground cover was gone—deep-rooted vegetation that would normally hold soil and moisture even during times of drought and high winds. As clear-cut forest couldn't mitigate floodwaters, grass-stripped prairies couldn't handle prolonged drought. Unanchored soil turned to dust. Winds whipped that dust into huge dark frenzies that often blackened the sky. Farms failed, driving thousands of Great Plains homesteaders farther west.

Though the Rockies begin in British Columbia, this flight path takes you across their southernmost reaches in Arizona, where there's lots of red earth and exposed shale, limestone, and sandstone. The lower Colorado River winds through the Grand Canyon and then takes a sharp downward turn near the Nevada-Arizona border, where the chalk white arch of the Hoover Dam impounds the turquoise sprawl of Lake Mead.

Flying due west now, we're passing over the tan expanses of the Mojave Desert. The first tentative dirt roads appear, along with the first small rectangles that signify human presence, however hermitlike. These faintly etched roads meet up with slightly thicker ones in simple intersections. Scattered rectangles scale up into isolated neighborhoods on the outskirts of the desert cities of Lancaster and Palmdale.

Once over the San Gabriel Mountains and into the Los Angeles Basin, though, there's dense human habitation—urban grids and suburban hives and freeways meeting freeways in increasingly complex joinery—all the way from the foothills to the coast. This "hardscape" obscures almost entirely the pre–twentieth-century L.A. River Watershed, once home to chinook salmon and rainbow trout.

The plane decelerates as it begins its descent into Los Angeles, but because everything is just a few hundred feet down below now, it goes by in streaks and you could be fooled into thinking you are actually going faster as you drop toward the runways of Los Angeles International Airport, which lie at the edges of the once vast wetlands of Santa Monica Bay.

(If these last few minutes of the flight had a sound track, it could well be the final, atonal crescendo of the Beatles' "A Day in the Life," which John Lennon had wanted to sound like "a tremendous build-up, from nothing up to something absolutely like the end of the world.")

Too often the story of our westward migration has been about human overreach, followed by the land's reactions and revenge.

EARTHBOUND

What you see of the Earth from an airplane window is an epic story involving big rivers and vast tracts of land, with the history of human impact showing up in broad, bold strokes. What you see from the ground is more like chamber music, the same story scaled down to the intimately local paths and actions of the people who have lived here.

Take Walker Creek and its immediate surroundings. Over more than forty years, we have covered just about every inch of it with our gaze and our bodies, from its beginnings in the sandy shallows between Conomo Point and Tommy Island to its source in the hills of West Gloucester.

It splits off from the Essex River and loops through marsh meadow for about a mile (as the minnow swims, not as the crow flies) before meeting its first significant human intervention, the remains of Haskell's gristmill. All you can see of it now are boulders spanning the creek, with a few posts that once formed the foundation of the mill. The boulders still form a rough fifteen-foot-long flume, though, and if you happen to be swimming toward it, your body will pick up speed as it approaches the opening, which seems narrower, more jagged, and more perilous to the unprotected human body the closer you get to it. You stiffen to avoid banging your knees or elbows against stone. (If you're in a kayak, the hull might hit a boulder or two.)

A few hundred feet farther upriver, there's another intervention: the Concord Street bridge, a stone box culvert with a metal grid over it, too narrow for two cars to pass over at the same time. Underneath, in the water—again, if you happened to be swimming or kayaking through—you'll find it's instantly a little cooler. If a car passes overhead, the grate clanks twice: ka-*chonk*, ka-*chonk*.

Past Concord Street and branching off to the right is a channel too straight to be natural; it seems to have been dug by preindustrial farmers wanting to get their goods down the Essex River to Gloucester and beyond, faster than their competition. Time—back then as much as today—is money.

The creek squiggles through marsh for another half mile until it meets the much smaller Walker Street bridge. This far upriver, it's no more than six feet wide, long past the point where, if you were swimming, you'd have turned around. A quarter mile farther, the saltwater creek has turned to freshwater, the marsh grass replaced by cattails. A hundred feet farther and Walker Creek is no more than a boulder-strewn brook. It is also traveling gradually uphill. The creek narrows further; you begin ducking under low-hanging branches.

Bracketed by Lincoln Street to your right (west) and Sumner Street to your left (east), the creek appears to halt at a steep bank, the roadbed of Route 133. You'd have to be mucking around in those woods at the bottom of the highway embankment to see for yourself that Walker Creek does not end here; it forks. One fork veers east, passing under a small culvert beneath Sumner Street, and ends in the hills to the east of there. The other fork continues across Route 133 through a much larger culvert embedded in the roadway. Here are the remains of the stone-lined flume for Henry Walker's sawmill, which once cut the oaks and hemlocks from nearby land, producing the boards that would become Cape Ann's houses and barns and schooners. This was leading-edge technology—these chutes, wheels, axles, grinding stones, and blades—back when these waterways were more important to the economy than roads.

Now, though, the presence of the highway is overwhelming, the swish and rumble of traffic blocking any creek sounds. Like many other state highways, 133 is an amalgam of local roads, and has been beefed up over the years to make it smooth, wide, and continuous from Gloucester to Andover. When you're on it, it shrinks time and space; that's the point of highways, after all. (And how much more the channels that move us at something like the speed of light, the channels made of silicon, the sixth most common element in the universe?)

The creek contains a mini-history of pre- and early-industrial technology. But it also contains this disconnect between technologies that scaled easily to the human body and those that vastly outpaced it. The young Karl Marx wrote of the alienation of people from the fruits of their labor, but more ultimately from their *Gattungswesen*, their "species-essence." We are nearly two centuries past these early manifestations of industrialization that so dismayed the young Marx, but his articulation of the problem—if not his political solutions—is as relevant as ever.

This is not theoretical. I am actually here, bushwhacking, ducking under and around saplings, climbing over the tumbled-down remains of the sawmill. Balancing on a boulder now, I stretch to see inside the five-foot-diameter corrugated-steel pipe running under the highway. It is both a juncture and a disjuncture.

Just a little water trickles through; there's a dam and a reservoir less than a mile upstream.

I emerge up above on Lincoln Street, brushing twigs and dirt from my sweater and jeans, stomping mud from my boots, relieved that nobody has seen me being eccentric here in this hidden place.

But, *rats*. Someone's out for a walk, coming this way.

It's our poet friend, Mark Stevick, which makes everything suddenly okay. He lives on this street with his wife and two children. He is also a professor of creative writing at a nearby college.

"Hey," he says.

"Hey," I respond. "I've been checking out the old sawmill down in there."

"Ah, I love that stuff, too."

Both of us, it seems, are chasing after metaphors.

SWIMMING TO THE TOP OF THE TIDE

At nose level in a saltwater creek, your cupped hands cutting through water the way the snout of a plane cuts through the atmosphere, the horizon is usually only a few feet away. The vanishing point is a canyonlike wall of very firm mud and a dense bamboo forest of grass. Because of the way these tidal creeks twist and turn, there is always something up ahead you can't see: a cormorant or an egret taking off, fingerling fish darting into shade just as you round the corner.

Sometimes you can swim with the current to the top of the tide, to the pause between flow and ebb. The water will begin to cover all but the top foot or so of the cordgrass—less if it's a "low" high tide, more if it's a "high" high tide. Your body is suspended in green-gold inner space as hay flecks swirl slowly all around you. The water no longer feels like water, exactly. It could be air, clouds, a gel.

This is what the "tide turning" looks and feels like when you're in it and it's not just a metaphor. You're at the apex of a bell curve as rendered in tide logs, at the height of an inhalation. A pause, a holding of breath, and then the beginnings of the long six-and-a-half-hour exhalation.

Or more accurately, the *apparent* pause. The Earth is still turning and gravity is still pulling, so what happens with the tide is not a full stop. But in that one spot—and that is all a body can inhabit at a time—you experience it as stillness. The horizon circles you. The jet trails arc. You are freshly aware of what is always the case: that your body goes about its business on a curved surface.

Tides, like all cycles of nature, are a precarious equilibrium of constants and variables. The constants are the gravitational relationships among the Earth, the Moon, and the Sun. Spring tides occur twice a month—regardless of the season—when Earth, Sun, and Moon line up straight, when the gravitational pull of the Moon and Sun on the Earth and its oceans are at their strongest. In our latitude, these high tides are in the ten- to ten-and-a-half-foot range.

A "spring perigee" tide is the scientific name for what we informally call king tides. They occur when a spring tide coincides with a perigee moon—that semiannual point in the Moon's elliptical orbit when it is closest to the Earth. In northern New England, spring perigee tides can surpass twelve feet—about two and a half to three feet higher than the mean high tide level.

These planetary constants can be predicted accurately far into the future, as well as reconstructed far

into the past. We can know exactly when spring perigee tides will happen in Gloucester a thousand years
from now, and can reconstruct when they happened a
thousand years ago, when the only human inhabitants
of the Essex River Basin were the Native Americans of
the Agawam region.

We cannot, however, predict exactly how high
those future tides will be, because the variables are,
well, variable. A warming Earth also means warmer
oceans. Warmer water both expands in volume and
evaporates at a greater rate than cooler water. Steamy
air is the fuel that causes storms to turn into hurricanes. Warming oceans, then, set the stage for increasingly frequent major storms.

And then there's the truly wild-card factor of ice-sheet
melt. It's happening at an accelerating rate, but exactly
when some massive chunk will break off, or "calve," is not
an exact science. In 2019, for example, a record-breaking
heat wave in Europe migrated west to Greenland, leading
to a 217-billion-ton ice loss—that's an area four times the
size of Manhattan, and enough water to keep taps flowing in the United States for 120 days.

Additionally, strong onshore winds and pressure
changes from a coastal storm can push an average high
tide considerably higher, resulting in a storm surge
that can swamp low-lying roads and bridges during a
nor'easter. In our family archives is home-movie evidence of one such nor'easter: Hurricane Gloria, which

hit eastern Massachusetts on September 27, 1985. Robert is the eye behind the camera, capturing jumpy footage of three of our friends, who are tromping around gleefully in floodwaters that have entirely flooded the Concord Street bridge over Walker Creek. Off in the distance, you can just make out a pickup truck inching through water up to its wheel wells.

Destructive as it was, Gloria did not coincide with particularly high tides. Had it occurred during a perigean spring tide, storm surge might have approached that of the Ash Wednesday storm of 1962, which flooded the entire East Coast from the Carolinas to Cape Cod. Or, more recently, Hurricane Sandy, which for eleven days wrought havoc from Cuba to Canada, including thirteen feet of storm surge that flooded the streets and subways of lower Manhattan.

In my life span so far, global sea level has risen a little over seven inches, a rate of approximately eleven inches per one hundred years. The most conservative estimates project a slight increase in that rate, to about 12.5 inches per hundred years—about one-eighth inch per year. But other estimates are higher, suggesting that the increase could reach 6.5 feet by 2100, an average of just under an inch per year.

I will not be alive in 2100, though my grandchildren probably will be. If some of our descendants travel to the North Shore at the turn of the century to visit the Hanlon family ancestral home, the coastline will be somewhere between modestly and drastically different from the one we've known in our forty years here.

By then, high tides could average anywhere from ten to sixteen feet; spring perigee tides could range from thirteen to eighteen feet. If the higher predictions hold, the Walker Creek bridge (currently about three and a half feet above sea level) would long since have been replaced by a bridge with a higher span. Regular sixteen-foot high tides could also mean the disappearance of portions of the Great Marsh, if the marsh's ability to build itself up is greatly outpaced by the rate of sea-level rise.

And yet sea-level rise is part of a much longer arc of human interventions in the Earth's biological, chemical, and geological processes. It began in prehistory, when humans first mastered fire. It built more rapidly during the Industrial Revolution of the eighteenth and nineteenth centuries, then spiked in a post–World War II "Great Acceleration." Fossil-fuel consumption increased exponentially, and wartime technologies were reimagined—and reengineered—to produce consumer products. Increasingly, the Earth's carbon reserves were not just being burned as fuel but spun into a stunning array of new materials, structures, and containers. These innovations both extended the natural reach of the human body and narrowed the gap between human desire and its fulfillment.

So many of these petroleum-based products are undeniably useful—like our wetsuits. These sleek second skins are a synthetic rubber made from a colorless liquid, chloroprene, which has the chemical formula C_4H_5Cl— four parts carbon, five parts hydrogen, and one part chlorine. The manufacturing process turns chloroprene molecules—or monomers—into a polymer—that is, into a chain of molecules connected to one another by chemical bonds. But too many petroleum-based concoctions fulfill short-lived human desires. Even worse, they remain as harmful flotsam in the biosphere—long after they've served their ephemeral purposes.

This book is an account of exploring one small ecosystem, one fractal bit of the worldwide system of coastal estuaries. But it's equally about being human creatures in an environment—fractal parts, if you will, of anthropogenic alterations to the Earth. The swimming practice began with gear, after all, with a pair of swim fins that, along with layers of neoprene, took us to places our unaided bodies could not otherwise have gone.

The Great Acceleration is our story in a larger, sociocultural sense, as well. Robert was born in 1953, and I in 1954—the year when births in the United States topped four million for the first time. It was seven years after the signing of the Paris Treaties ending World War II, and two years before President Dwight

Eisenhower would sign the Federal Aid Highway Act, which funded the construction of some forty thousand miles of new highways. In 1954, Atomic Energy Commission Chairman Lewis Strauss expressed the exuberant confidence of the times:

> Transmutation of the elements—unlimited power, [the] ability to investigate the working of living cells by tracer atoms, the secret of photosynthesis about to be uncovered—these and a host of other results all in 15 short years. It is not too much to expect that our children will enjoy in their homes electrical energy too cheap to meter, will know of great periodic regional famines in the world only as matters of history, will travel effortlessly over the seas and under them and through the air with a minimum of danger and at great speeds, and will experience a lifespan far longer than ours, as disease yields and man comes to understand what causes him to age. This is the forecast for an age of peace.

But in the same year, French sociologist Jacques Ellul published *The Technological Society,* in which he took a much dimmer view of this "age of peace." Technology would not liberate "modern man" but, rather, imprison him:

. . . there is "no exit"; he cannot pierce the shell of technology again to find the ancient milieu to which he was adapted for hundreds of thousands of years. . . . In our cities there is no more day or night or heat or cold. But there is overpopulation, thralldom to press and television, total absence of purpose. All men are constrained by means external to them to ends equally external. The further the technical mechanism develops that allows us to escape natural necessity, the more we are subjected to artificial technical necessities.

Hoover Dam, the massive concrete arch-gravity dam set into the Black Canyon of the Colorado River, has become a kind of archetype for me.

In the mid-1990s, my mother lived in nearby Henderson, Nevada. She and I took a tour of the dam together once, but I went by myself several times as well, drawn back for reasons I couldn't fully understand at the time.

Though I'm not mechanically inclined, I wanted to know how the thing worked. I gathered facts and specs, researching the path of the water from Lake Mead into the rectangular mouths of twin intake towers behind the dam's curved headwall, then through underground penstocks to the two hydroelectric power plants at the dam's base—one on the Arizona side of the Colorado River, the other on the Nevada side. The water's force turns hydraulic turbines that, in turn, rotate a series of generators, capturing four billion kilowatt hours of electricity each year, powering substantial parts of Nevada, Arizona, and Southern California.

I have stood at the viewing stations built into the dam's crest, awestruck by the headwall's 726-foot descent to the bottom. The river, a foam-marbled viridian, continues south, winding through the steep basalt walls of the canyon. This is a charged, fraught zone, where nature meets technology in ways both visible and invisible.

Every once in a while I'll have a dream about swimming toward the water shooting out of the turbines at the base of the dam—a megaversion of the bodysurfing wipeouts of my Southern California childhood.

Until recently, I did not fully realize that the Colorado River pretty much halts at the United States–Mexico border. What was once Mexico's fertile Colorado River Delta has been mostly dry riverbed for nearly eighty years, petering out in the Sonoran Desert at the base of the Sierra de Juárez, long before its natural end point in the Sea of Cortez.

At the border, the Imperial Dam diverts nearly all of the southern Colorado River into the All-American Canal, an eighty-mile aqueduct that runs like a wall along the Mexico-California border. Like the many other aqueducts in the arid Southwest, the canal is a striking human mark, a thin blue line edged crisply with white, scoring the light sand of southeastern California.

In the abstract, it's a beautiful thing.

From the air, if you didn't know its backstory, the depleted Colorado River Delta has its own austere beauty: ghostlike fans and swirls etched into the desert, reaching toward the azure waters of the Sea of Cortez. What is left of the Colorado River in Mexico is a shadow, a presence of absence.

And beauty can sometimes be terrible.

I've been formed by other archetypes as well, especially those that speak to our poignant sense of the gap between what our world is and what it ought to be. There is a recurring yearning, in both Jewish and Christian thought, for *apokatastasis,* for the redemption and restoration not just of individuals but of the entire cosmos.

One of the most compelling, in my estimation, is the prophet Ezekiel's vision of the restored temple in Jerusalem, the Heavenly City. He describes a great river "coming out from under the threshold of the temple toward the east," flowing toward the Dead Sea, turning the salty water there fresh. Trees grow on either side of the river, trees whose "fruit will serve for food and their leaves for healing." The vision of redemption continues in a rhapsody:

Swarms of living creatures will live wherever the river flows. There will be large numbers of fish, because this water flows there and makes the salt water fresh; so where the river flows everything will live. Fishermen will stand along the shore; from En Gedi to En Eglaim there will be places for spreading nets. The fish will be of many kinds—like the fish of the Mediterranean Sea. . . .

Many years after Ezekiel's prophetic vision in the late fifth century BCE, John of Patmos, an early Christian, was also in exile, banished by the Roman emperor Domitian to a small, rocky island off the coast of Turkey. In what may have been his lonely despair, John recalls Ezekiel's vision of the New Jerusalem, of "the river of the water of life, bright as crystal." But then he adds something that I expect will inform my sense of vocation for the rest of my life: "And the leaves of the trees are for the healing of nations."

EPILOGUE
May 2020

The five acres of West Gloucester land we bought in 1979 have been good to us. Though we sold that first house and lived in nearby Essex for twenty-five years, we kept most of the land and built a barn on it, where the furniture for our business was made.

In 2016, Robert and two friends began the arduous process of rebuilding the barn as our retirement home. In 2017, we moved back to our old neighborhood, this borough of wetlands, granite outcroppings, and woods. The converted barn still has plenty of workshop and studio space, where we continue to make things—paintings, furniture, sculpture, and, most recently, this book.

Artists don't retire (and I mean the word in the broad sense of "makers"). There are many makers here—musicians, visual artists, sculptors, photographers, poets, science writers, landscape designers, and artisans of all kinds. Until a few years before her death at age ninety-four, neighborhood matriarch Ruth Soucy wove mesh liners for lobster traps. They are the functional part of the trap, but they're also beautiful basketlike enclosures.

This is the spring of the pandemic. We have been

biking, hiking, kayaking, and swimming more than we usually do. Even if we haven't got much time, we can always take a hike from our back door into the woods above the Great Ledge, the cliff of granite that runs from our property all the way to Walker Creek.

It isn't until the third week of May that spring finally, truly arrives in these woods. Wild lily of the valley bitmaps the forest floor in pointillist beauty, most strikingly in the low light of early morning or late evening. Since the beginning of May, the oak, maple, birch, and beech have been budding, but only in the last few days have they really unfurled. Beech is dominant here, not just by being the first to unfold but also by the sheer volume and intensity of that unfolding. Beech leaves are a brilliant chartreuse, soft as chamois cloth, the size of a small human hand. Their branches stretch very horizontally, filling the airspace with green.

We're following an ancient path, gnarly with exposed tree roots, that winds along the top of the Great Ledge. In the winter months, it's easy to see the marsh eighty feet down, but now, as we walk, we just see patches of it through slots in the green. The marsh lawn looks pale and sere by comparison, the lavender-tan of last year's grass still the dominant color, with the new growth just a haze.

A man in jeans and a hooded sweatshirt is coming our way. He has light brown hair and a face I almost recognize. He steps aside a bit to let us pass at a safe distance. We nod a greeting but don't stop to talk. People tend to like their solitude in these woods. It's only a few minutes later that I realize that he's the middle son of neighbors who live over on Walker Street. I last saw him when he was a teenager, but he must be close to forty now, older than his parents were when we first met them. Maybe he's home from some big city or other, riding out the pandemic.

There's a sense, this spring, of time suspended—or of all times being present. Human settlement has always been sparse here, but it would be crowded if everyone who'd ever lived in this neighborhood gathered all at once. And that's not even counting the animals—these woods are interlaced with the faint pathways of untold generations of white-tailed deer. Eight hundred years ago, the Algonquin began using and thickening the deer paths that corresponded with their fishing and farming. Five hundred years later, the first English settlers wove straighter and wider paths to accommodate their carts and horses. In the middle of the twentieth century, Bostonians and other newcomers arrived, buying up old farmhouses and building new ones. Some of these newcomers, like us, walked the woods, but their walking by then was mainly recreational.

We've been hiking through greenbelt land, but now we are crossing over into private property again, an eleven-acre peninsula sloping down to the marsh, thick with greenbrier, low-bush blueberry, and granite.

It was bought in the early 1960s by what was then the Massachusetts Electric Company, but it has never been developed.

A few months ago, someone built a small shelter at the highest part of the land. Architecturally, the structure falls somewhere between a tepee and a yurt, minus any exterior sheathing. Robert and I duck inside, sheltered for a few minutes by interlacing oak branches that soar over us like a rustic version of cathedral arches.

Downhill toward the marsh now. We stand on boulders, perched above the creek, where it's low tide, just a glistening trickle of water. Robert points out some large stones in the creek, enough of a line that he can imagine them as the remains of a farmer's bridge.

"Do you want to walk back on the marsh or go back the way we came?" he asks.

"The marsh," I say. I always prefer walking a loop to backtracking. We will head home on the very rough trail that runs along the bottom of the Great Ledge. We pause at a salt panne that has always seemed too perfectly round to have been naturally formed. Its feathery perimeter looks womblike. Most of the small inhabitants dart into shade when they feel our footsteps, but I spot an inch-long crustacean that we decide is probably a lobster, and a fish that, at two inches, has already taken on its adult proportions.

"I wonder if they're stuck here," I muse, then remember that the upcoming new-moon tide will cover the marsh lawn with a skim of seawater and render this impoundment irrelevant. These creatures will easily make their way to Walker Creek, and eventually out into Ipswich Bay and the Atlantic Ocean.

The Ledge trail runs alongside an offshoot of Walker Creek. Only a few feet wide here, it passes invisibly through a dense stand of reeds, and ends in the boggy part of our land, downhill from our house. On the west side of the property, a similar offshoot of Lufkin Creek nearly meets up with this last bit of Walker Creek. On maps, it's usually rendered as a continuous small waterway. But it's seldom wet enough for that to be accurate. Most of the time, this is an enchantingly indeterminate zone of hummocks and little pools, swamp maple, bog fern, and yellow iris.

We have been borrowing species that grow wild here, relocating them in the parts of the land we disrupted to put in a septic system and well. We are required to mitigate that loss by replanting an equivalent area in native species. So far, we've rehomed a lot of low-bush blueberry, ferns, and lupine, and planted juniper, dogwood, and other native trees. The idea is to fill back in at least some of the forest canopy that we've taken away by living here.

It's such a minuscule act of stewardship. What we are practicing are small acts of remediation, not restoration.

But we do so because it's an act of faith in the Commons—the ancient yet ever-new idea that the resources of the land ultimately belong to all of us.

ACKNOWLEDGMENTS

Heartfelt thanks to Erika Goldman and Bellevue Literary Press, for promoting books exploring the fertile territories where the arts and sciences intersect.

I am deeply grateful to those who provided help of all kinds. Thank you, Tuesday Writing Group: Cynthia Linkas, Anne Emerson, Miriam Weinstein, Laura Wainwright, Elizabeth Berges, Margaret Carlton-Foss, and Michal Brownell. Thank you, Anne Pelikan, Susan Quateman, Bruce Herman, Ann Smith, William Craig, and Mark Sargent, for your insights and encouragement. Thank you, Dorothy Boorse and Anne Giblin, for taking the time to be interviewed and helping me fact-check my science. Thank you, Tim Traver, Deborah Cramer, William Sargent, Lynne Cox, and Julia Glass, for reading and providing comments on my book.

I owe special debts of love to:

Sally Ryder Brady, writing teacher and agent extraordinaire, without whom this book might never have reached the finish line.

Karen O'Keefe, whose gift of those Bahamas getaways afforded me, year after year, much peaceful writing time.

The Reverend Martha Giltinan (1957–2014), whose earthy spirituality and love for the natural world were formative for me.

Mary Hanlon, beloved daughter, who believed in this book and devoted many hours to helping me hone both its prose and its vision.

Robert Hanlon, my swimming and absolutely everything else buddy for all these many years.

ENDNOTES

Land and Sea: An Overture

p. 16: "The East Coast turns a corner . . ."
The 20,000-year-old, 2,300-square-mile Barnes Ice
Cap (on Baffin Island in Nunavut, Canada) is all
that is left of the Laurentide Ice Sheet.

p. 18: "As we swam into the winter . . ."
Wendell Berry, *The Unforeseen Wilderness:
Kentucky's Red River Gorge* (Lexington: University
of Kentucky Press, 1971), 43.

p. 19: "It is about how the habit . . ." David Abram,
quoted by Lynn Margulis in the chapter "Living
by Gaia," in Jonathan White, *Talking on the Water:
Conversations about Nature and Creativity* (San
Antonio: Trinity University Press, 2016), 71.

Tidelog

p. 45: "I knew all of this because . . ." www.tidelog.com.

September

p. 50: "Every one of us occupies . . ." Abraham Joshua
Heschel, *The Sabbath* (New York: Farrar, Straus
and Giroux, 1951), 87.

Biologist

p. 51: "Dorothy Boorse is a biology professor . . ."
Dorothy Boorse and Richard Wright, *Environmental
Science: Toward a Sustainable Future* (New York:
Pearson, 2013).

p. 53: "In Louisiana, nearly two thousand . . ." An average of 34 square miles of South Louisiana land, mostly marsh, has disappeared each year for the past five decades, according to the U.S. Geological Survey.

Cold

p. 59: *"Fit is a very important aspect . . ."* The italic passage here and subsequent ones in this chapter are from "How to Choose a Wetsuit," available at www.evo.com.

January

p. 92: "A few days later . . ." The condos had been built near the end of the New England real estate boom of the late 1980s. The subsequent economic downturn caught the developer with houses half built and no more money to complete the project. Everything was sold back to the bank, which sold it to another developer—except for the one-acre "barn lot" that became the site, for 25 years, of our owner-occupied business, Walker Creek Furniture.

p. 96: "The further into the future . . ." Chloë N. Duckworth, "The Archaeology of the Future, Part 2," *Heritage Daily,* January 3, 2014, available at www.heritagedaily.com/2014/01/ the-archaeology-of-the-future-part-2/56891.

Swimming in Parentheses

p. 99: "I'm not acclimated to this. . . ." Anthony Tommasini, "Robert Lurtsema, 68, Champion of Classical Music on the Radio," *New York Times,* June 16, 2020.

p. 99: "I don't think there's anything wrong . . ." Kat Eschner, "Tales of the Doomed Franklin Expedition Long Ignored the Inuit Side, But 'The Terror' Flips the Script," *Smithsonian*, April 6, 2018, available at www.smithsonianmag.com/arts- culture/heres-how-amc-producers-worked-inuit- fictionalized-franklin-expedition-show-180968643/.

Quarry

p. 102: "described by local historian Barbara Erkkila
. . ." Barbara Erkkila, *Hammers on Stone: A History
of Cape Ann Granite* (Woolwich, ME: TBW
Books, 1980), 4.

p. 108: "Once adopted, though . . ." Dyson's lecture was
later published as the chapter "Quick is Beautiful"
in his book *Infinite in All Directions* (New York:
Harper & Row, 1988), 137.

Late Winter

p. 112: "Seaweed has long been used . . ." from "Is
Seaweed Alone Sufficient to Ward off Scurvy?"
Comment by Squink on The Straight Dope
Message Board https://boards.straightdope.
com/t/is-seaweed-alone-sufficient-to-ward-off-
scurvy/413597/2.

p. 112: "Glasswort is also edible . . ." from
"GlasswortGalore," http://www.eattheweeds.com/
salicornia-bigelovii-2/.

The Return of Green

pp. 118–119: "At home, I googled . . ." from "Adding
Water," undated post in Valve Developer
Community website, available at developer.
valvesoftware.com/wiki/Adding_Water.

Full Circle

p. 133: "The same suits that transformed . . ." William
F. Byrne, *Edmund Burke for Our Time: Moral
Imagination, Meaning and Politics* (Dekalb:
Northern Illinois University Press, 2011), loc. 169
(Kindle version). Burke's original mention of the
term appears in *Reflections on the Revolution in
France* (1790). A recent printing is *Reflections on the
Revolution in France*, ed. L. G. Mitchell (Oxford:
Oxford University Press, 2009), 77.

Ground Truth

p. 139: "Flipping through the . . ." The "Big Here" quiz, written by Peter Warshall, first appeared in the 1975 edition of the *Whole Earth Catalog,* but it has been revised and added to many times since then. I'm not sure which version we were reading in 1979.

p. 147: "Preserving effective . . ." The Blue Carbon Initiative, "Mitigating Climate Change through Coastal Ecosystem Management," available at www.thebluecarboninitiative.org.

Nassau, Again

p. 157: "Here it's not hard . . ." Lynn Margulis and Dorion Sagan, *Microcosmos: Four Billion Years of Microbial Evolution* (Berkeley: University of California Press, 1997), 176.

Areas of Critical Environmental Concern

p. 161: "Then there are the diminishments . . ." Deborah Cramer, *Great Waters: An Atlantic Passage* (New York: Norton, 2002), 309.

pp. 162–163: "The Great Marsh has many . . ." Taj Schottland, Melissa G. Merriam, Christopher Hilke, Kristen Grubbs, and Wayne Castonguay, "Great Marsh Coastal Adaptation Plan," December 1, 2017, available at www.nwf.org/greatmarshadaptation.

p. 164: "I stumbled on this information . . ." Gordon Harris, "Nuclear Ipswich: 1967–1970," Historic Ipswich, 2014, available at historicipswich.org/2020/01/16/nuclear-ipswich/.

pp. 167–168: "In the late 1960s . . ." John D. Fogg, *Recollections of a Salt Marsh Farmer* (Seabrook, NH: Historical Society of Seabrook, 1983), 4.

pp. 168–169: "What followed was . . ." In my family archives is a home movie taken by my father in 1960, a panoramic view from the roof of our house in Camarillo, California. Five miles to the west, you can just make out the sparkling blue line of the Pacific Ocean. To the east are rolling hills studded with live oaks. Something the movie couldn't possibly have shown is a 2,800-acre laboratory tucked away in a remote region of Simi Valley, just eighteen miles from Camarillo. The Santa Susana Field Laboratory was a collaboration between the U.S. government and private companies to test the uses of nuclear power. On July 12, 1959, the SSFL's sodium reactor had experienced a "criticality incident," an uncontrolled nuclear-fission chain reaction, which released approximately 260 times more radiation into the environment than the Three Mile Island accident, still twenty years in the future. The incident remained a state secret until nearly half a century later.

Channels

pp. 171–172: "If there's no traffic . . ." Mihaly Csikszentmihalyi, "Go with the Flow," interview by John Geirland, *Wired*, September 1, 1996, available at www.wired.com/1996/09/czik/.

p. 173: "We are many miles . . ." from "Louisiana: State Energy Profile," U.S. Energy Information Administration, 2017, available at www.eia.gov/state/?sid=LA.

p. 178: "Chelsea Creek is the source . . ." from NOAH's old (archived) website https://noahcdc.org/sites/oldsite/cbe/ccrp.html#:~:text=Chelsea%20 Creek%20is%20the%20source,of%20East%20 Boston%20and%20Chelsea.&text=In%20 addition%2C%20Chelsea%20Creek%20is,of%20 water%20in%20the%20Commonwealth.

p. 178: "According to Professors Daniel Faber and . . ." Daniel Faber and Eric Krieg, "Unequal Exposure to Ecological Hazards," *Environmental Health Perspectives* 110 (April 2002): 277–288, available at www.ncbi.nih.gov/pmc/articles/PMC1241174/.

p. 181: "I pull my phone from . . ." from "Mill Creek Riverwalk," City of Chelsea, Massachusetts, available at www.chelseama.gov/parks-playgrounds/pages/mill-creek-riverwalk/.

Airborne

p. 190: "When my father worked . . ." Susan Scott Parrish, "The Great Mississippi Flood of 1927 Laid Bare the Divide Between the North and the South," *Smithsonian,* April 11, 2017, available at www.smithsonianmag.com/history/devastating-mississippi-river-flood-uprooted-americas-faith-progress-180962856/.

pp. 190–191: "During the same era . . ." See Pare Lorentz's *The Plow That Broke the Plains* (U.S. documentary film, 1936) and *The River* (U.S. documentary film, 1938).

p. 192: "If these last few minutes . . ." Walter Everett, *The Beatles as Musicians: Revolver Through the Anthology* (New York: Oxford University Press, 1999), 118.

Swimming to the Top of the Tide

p. 200: "And then there's the truly wild-card . . ." Christine Dell'Amore, "Ice Island Breaks off Greenland, Bigger Than Manhattan," August 8, 2010, available at www.nationalgeographic.com/news/2010/8/100806-ice-chunk-island-greenland-glacier-petermann-biggest-science/.

p. 204: "Transmutation of the elements . . ." Lewis L. Strauss, "Remarks Prepared for Delivery at the Founder's Day Dinner, National Association of Science Writers," September 16, 1954, available at www.nrc.gov/docs/ML1613/ML16131A120.pdf.

p. 205: ". . . there is 'no exit'; he cannot . . ." Jacques Ellul, *The Technological Society*, trans. John Wilkinson (New York: Alfred A. Knopf, 1964), 428.

Epilogue

pp. 211–212: "We've been hiking through . . ." When we bought the Essex barn that would house the retail part of our business, it had never been anything but a barn. You could see slits of the outdoors through its siding. A blind man, Earl Goodwin, had supported his family in that barn by caning chairs. The barn was full of stuff, including many boxes of old papers, one of which was overflowing with news clippings, blueprints, and records of court hearings involving the Massachusetts Electric Company back in the late 1960s. We pulled out the largest of the blueprints, stunned by something that could have happened but didn't: power lines all the way across the Great Marsh from West Gloucester to Seabrook, New Hampshire. Electrical towers are built about a thousand feet apart, and we can make an educated guess that one of them might have gone up somewhere very near the stick hut we saw on our walk that spring day in 2020. History is about what happened, but it's also about what didn't happen.

BELLEVUE LITERARY PRESS is devoted to publishing
literary fiction and nonfiction at the intersection of
the arts and sciences because we believe that science
and the humanities are natural companions for
understanding the human experience. We feature
exceptional literature that explores the nature of
perception and the underpinnings of the social contract.
With each book we publish, our goal is to foster a rich,
interdisciplinary dialogue that will forge new tools for
thinking and engaging with the world.

To support our press and its mission,
and for our full catalogue of published titles,
please visit us at blpress.org.

BELLEVUE LITERARY PRESS
New York